THERE'S ALWAYS MORE FUN TO BE HAD!

JAY BARRATT

PAGE PUBLISHING, INC.
Conneaut Lake, PA

First originally published by Page Publishing 2021

ISBN 978-1-6624-4672-6 (pbk)
ISBN 978-1-6624-4673-3 (digital)

Printed in the United States of America

CONTENTS

ACKNOWLEDGMENTS

This is dedicated to my friends who have shared in many of these events and are responsible for the many laughs I've had on the road over the years:

- Wesley "Gabby" Karlson
- Paul J. Cropper
- David Lango
- Tony Kush
- The other men and women of the Rogue Hogs

This is dedicated as well to my wife, Stacey, who has been both my road and life partner and who nursed me back to health after both potentially fatal motorcycle crashes that I have endured.

Also, I am thankful for the physical therapy professionals at Canyon Therapy in Cody, Wyoming, where I have become—unwittingly—a returning customer since 2007!

Lastly, I want to acknowledge the editing staff at Page Publishing. Their attention to details, and adherence to standards should yield a more enjoyable experience for you—my readers.

INTRODUCTION

The following collection of short stories chronicles events I have experienced while on two wheels—first on a bicycle, then on motorcycles—over a fifty-year span. While these motorcyclist-centric tales have garnered the attention of my over-the-road friends, many of my non-riding friends have told me they have enjoyed reading them too. So whether you are a hard-core Harley enthusiast or an armchair jockey only, hopefully you might find this collection interesting enough to read from start to finish.

This compilation is a work in progress because there's always more fun to be had—and worth writing about!

About Writing

After reading some of my online social media posts describing experiences from the saddle of my Harleys, certain friends would tell me, "You ought to write a book." I did that very thing—384 pages, entitled *Perpetual Motion*. Despite surviving reviewer redlines, I balked at publishing that for certain reasons on which I won't elaborate now; I'll revisit it someday. This collection of tales from two wheels, however, will have to suffice for my friends' call to "write a book," at least for now.

Am I a good writer? I have no idea. While all writers need an editor, I do know that I am a better writer than I would otherwise have been were it not for a deal I made with my grandmother fifty years ago and a concurrent deal I made with my parents to earn my first two-wheeled mode of transportation—my prized purple Kent Sting-Ray bicycle, 1970 vintage.

Except during tenth grade, I was on the honor roll all but one grading period throughout high school. Back in grade school, however, I was an average student at best. My grades followed a cycle of As and Bs followed by Cs and Ds. Back then, my classrooms included as many as fifty-eight students in a single room with a single teacher.

Because of the large class size, we would switch seats periodically. That is, the kids in the back of the room would move up gradually while those who started up front moved to the back row. While I had never made the correlation back then, I later came to realize that when I sat up front, my grades were respectable, but while in the back of the classroom, not so much.

That had nothing to do with me screwing off while removed from the watchful eye of the teacher while I was seated in the back of the room—well…maybe a little! The real problem though was that I simply couldn't see the blackboard—I needed glasses. I learned that too late. It wasn't until I had started driving in high school when I realized my eyes weren't as good as most of my classmates'.

So when I was nine years old, it was no surprise to me that I barely got two Ds and four Cs on my first report card for the year while seated at the back of the room. The worst part was, we had to get report cards signed by our parents, and I hadn't yet perfected forging my mother's signature.

The shit hit the fan when the folks learned that I had "earned" the Ds in math and English. I mean, really, who the hell could diagram a sentence or do long division without following what was being written on the blackboard?

Back then, my parents attributed poor performance only to lack of motivation. Poor eyesight wasn't on their radar.

What made that ass-chewing worse was that my parents unloaded on me in front of my grandmother—I was embarrassed. Luckily for me I had one of those shrewd grandmothers who knew the importance of education and how to motivate a nine-year-old.

Grandmother took me aside and offered me a deal. She knew that in order to get good at anything, you must practice. So she told me that if I kept a journal—and let her read it each time we visited—she would pay me twenty-five cents each week. Twenty-five cents was a fortune to a nine-year-old, who could fill a small paper sack with penny candy. I wasn't all that keen on more "homework," which is how I viewed keeping a journal, but the prospect of abundant candy was quite enticing. I did the deal.

I had been pestering my parents throughout the preceding summer to buy me a bicycle—without the desired effect. My father, who was an artillery officer, knew the importance of math and also how to motivate me, despite lack of motivation not being the root cause of my bad grades.

When the emotional furor over my grades died down, Dad told me that I would get a new bicycle for Christmas, but only if I got at least a B in math and English on my next report card. The only thing standing between me and my shiny new bike was mastering long division and sentence diagrams from the back of the room—overcome by a simple twist of fate.

One morning before the bell rang, I and a friend were using the flagpole and lanyard to catapult small rocks out of sight over the building. We would stretch the flag lanyard as far as possible until the flagpole would bend slightly. We would then position small rocks next to the metal clip that held the flag and release them. The pole would spring back with enough force to catapult the rocks out of sight.

Unfortunately, what goes up must come down. One of our missiles found its way to the noggin of some second grader in the playground on the other side of the school. We were both convicted of "throwing" rocks.

My penalty? After a visit to the stationery closet with the principal and application of the "board of education" to my backside, I was required to sit in the "hot seat." The hot seat was right up front under the teacher's nose—a place of shame to be occupied by me until another student committed a more egregious offense than catapulting rocks from the flagpole. That never happened that year, and so for the rest of fourth grade, I enjoyed a reasonably clear, unobstructed view of the blackboard and finally got to see divisors and remainders and subjects and predicates.

Well, I'm here to tell you that this kid proudly took home his next report card—just before Christmas break—with four As and two Bs. And true to his word, the old man bought me my first bicycle.

And while today I'm convinced that my deal with my grandmother had nothing to do with my English improvement for that year—I was simply able to see the damn blackboard—I continued journaling only to keep the candy flowing. The one near-term result of "the deal" was my first cavity!

In the long run, however, I am convinced that my journaling improved my writing. So much so that when I took the advanced placement testing in senior year, I tested out of the six required college writing credits. And that was achieved despite the unethical actions of a hateful tenth-grade English teacher—more on that later.

Although I continued journaling, I stopped sharing with my grandmother despite her keeping pace with inflation. I was getting $1 for each read by the time I was sixteen. But by then, my life was getting interesting—no way did I want Granny learning that I had lost my virginity or about my first "murdercycle" ride. As far as she knew, I had simply quit writing by then.

What follows is a compilation of on-the-road tales crafted mostly from the pages of my journals, which I continue to fill to this day almost compulsively. Damn it, Granny, this is your fault!

THE TWO COLDEST RIDES

My first bicycle was a months-long carrot dangled before me by my shrewd father. The price? I had to pull my math and English grades up from a D to at least a B before Christmas break. The As that I earned also earned me a to-die-for purple Kent Sting-Ray* twenty-inch bike, complete with purple metal flake vinyl-covered banana seat, sissy bar, red pinstriped tires, and a "nut ripper" gear shifter, so called because it was mounted to the top tube of the frame and, I suppose, was responsible for the ultimate mutilation in a crash—at least in the mind of a ten-year-old boy.

I remember going obediently to bed early on Christmas Eve, ostensibly to ensure we wouldn't interfere with the Big Guy while eating the milk and cookies we left out for him before he got down to the serious business of covering the floor under the tree with presents. At ten, I was on the fence as to whether the Big Guy really existed, but no way did I want to chance it. I went to my room and stayed put despite being awoken twice by what I could have sworn were elves cussing.

Years later, I learned that my prized bicycle cost forty-five dollars. For five dollars more, Dunbar's Cyclery would have assembled it for Dad. No way would Dad stand for such blatant thievery. Instead, he assembled the bike himself with assistance possibly from some foul-mouthed elves.

You see, my father's father died when Dad was just six months old. He had no one to teach him how to turn a wrench. I'm sure he

---

* "Sting-Ray" was actually a trademark model of a Schwinn bicycle, but us kids all referred to any similar "banana" or "muscle" bike as a Sting-Ray, regardless of whether it was a Schwinn, Kent, Huffy, Raleigh, or any other brand.

must have been frustrated and exhausted in order for him to swear loud enough to wake me, but he overcame whatever challenges he faced to ensure I had a properly built set of wheels by morning. He delivered.

With the *possible* exception of losing my virginity, nothing gave me greater joy in my life, until I got married to Stacey, than seeing that gleaming Sting-Ray under the tree and knowing it was mine!

My brother and I loved and hated Christmas equally. We loved the presents we got but hated getting dressed up for church and the inevitable flood of adult relatives who would want to pull us away from our cool new stuff—*to talk*—for shit sakes! What ten-year-old should have to endure that?

I begged my mother to let me ride the Sting-Ray immediately, first thing on Christmas morning, knowing full well the answer would be no. From experience, I knew I had to start pestering her first thing so I could be certain of wearing her down by midafternoon. To my utter shock, Mom said, "After church, change out of your good clothes before you go riding."

I was stunned. She not only added hours of daylight to my day, she allowed me to shed the monkey suit before company arrived. She knew how much that bike meant to me and wasn't going to prolong the agonizing wait for that first ride. My characteristically rigid mom could be very cool like that in small doses.

Christmas day was frigid with high winds. The walk to church was brutal with the wind cutting through my knit slacks. I then had to endure the retelling of Jesus's birth in a story I had heard exactly the same way for each of the few years before. I got smacked on the hand no less than six times during mass for looking at Mom's watch. Did the Sting-Ray exist just to torture me?

When I finally arrived home, I raced upstairs, getting yelled at one more time for skipping every other step while full speed ahead. I threw my good clothes on the bed and grabbed a pair of jeans and a heavy crew neck sweater. At the last moment, I thought to put on long johns, but considering the long johns I had as a kid were either ineffective one-hundred-percent cold cotton or one-hundred-per-cent godawful itchy wool—which I dreaded wearing—I chose the cotton set and finished dressing. To avoid getting yelled at again for running down the steps, I slid down the bannister instead.

Just as the long johns of my youth left a lot to be desired, so did boys' outerwear. I only owned an ugly brown plaid wool coat that buttoned down the front. That plus the wool sweater would be my riding outfit for the day. And out the door I went, as happy as a pig in shit!

I only rode back and forth from the riverfront to my school—six blocks. The feeling of powering my own two-wheeled machine was exhilarating. I rode nonstop from about noon until the orange glow filled the late afternoon sky. I would have stayed out longer, but no way did I want to risk being late for Christmas dinner because I knew the only punishment at that point would be the loss of my riding privileges—well, for that reason and because I was cold, colder than I had ever been before.

By the time I got home, it was nearly dark, and I had started shaking uncontrollably. Earlier in the day, my hands were in agony from the cold, but I just pressed on. I wondered how much warmer I might have been if I had just owned a zip-front coat. As it was, the frigid air blew past the buttons, chilling me to the core. Hypothermia had set in.

After the obligatory hello to all our dinner guests, I raced to the kitchen to run warm water over my hands, which oddly had quit hurting about an hour before I came home. That was a big mistake. When the sensation returned to my hands, I was in agony!

The doctor confirmed the next day that I had gotten frostbite on most of my fingers and the flesh on my face under my eyes. That was the first real pain I had ever experienced. Still, despite the painful fingers and cheeks, I sat by the fireplace and stared at my bike after Christmas dinner while the bitter wind blew outside. It was really there, and I had *earned* it.

As was customary, we kids had the whole week off from school after Christmas, and I had planned to ride my bike every day. The weather warmed up nicely—into the forties. Despite that, I never rode my glorious Sting-Ray again until after we went back to school. The waxy frostbitten fingers that were slathered in salve and wrapped in gauze wouldn't allow me to even carry my bike outside, let alone ride it again for a while. That dose of irony was a tough pill to swallow!

That purple Kent bicycle I earned in 1970 was my prized possession until I was fourteen. By then, I had gotten the itch for a ten-speed. Eventually, at fifteen, I got the ten-speed that I wanted. And although on acquiring it, it seemed massively important, it just wasn't the same as that first bike. I parted with that Kent for $25, which I also "earned" because I had lavished care and maintenance on it. It was in tip-top mechanical condition. I learned to wrench by maintaining that bike and grew those skills on getting my first car and beyond, eventually tearing into Harley motors and transmissions. And along the way, I eventually acquired the proper clothes for riding in any weather!

After my frostbitten fingers eventually healed from that first ride, I rode that Sting-Ray everywhere. Mom didn't drive, so if I wanted to visit friends in the outlying neighborhoods, I'd carry what I needed, strapped to the handlebars or sissy bar, and head out. That bike was my freedom machine, as was the ten-speed that replaced it.

But with age comes wisdom. A *real* freedom machine is a rip-snortin' "Milwaukee Vibrator"—a Harley-Davidson V-twin thumping between your legs.

The first Harley I rode wasn't mine, although I had nearly uninhibited access to it for more than two years. Later, I acquired a 1964 Duo Glide—among the last of the Harley Panheads.

When I moved to Arizona in 1983, I divested myself of all large possessions—including my Duo Glide. Nevertheless, I did get some saddle time in occasionally on a friend's KZ-1000, but I was mostly off two wheels until 1991 when I bought my first new Harley after I left Arizona and had taken a job with DuPont in Delaware.

Despite a great paying job with DuPont, I couldn't afford a new Harley Big Twin. I settled for an XLH 1200 instead—the longest running Harley model, the Sportster. While the smallest Harley is still a big bike, I really wanted a Big Twin—a Softail or Dyna Glide.

Back when Harley was struggling in the 1970s, you could buy a brand-new Sportster, ride it for a year, and then trade up to a bigger Harley, and they would give you what you paid for the Sporty in trade. Ironically, while I could only get financing initially for the $6,800 Sportster, I was able to finance a new Big Twin less than a year later when I traded it in. The owner of Millville Harley-Davidson gave me what I paid for the Sporty in trade on a new Softail Springer, just like he had done to survive in the seventies. Because of the trade-in, the credit union allowed me to finance the $12,200 Big Twin. I never understood the logic for that because I had almost no equity in the Sportster, but I wasn't going to let that keep me from upgrading where the credit union was on board.

Around that same time, I had moved into an apartment with no place to keep a bike other than on the street—a risky proposition. So I asked the old man if I could keep the new bike in one of his garages. Despite his dislike for "murdercycles," he gave me the go-ahead. Back then, Dad lived in Smyrna, about thirty-five miles from my apartment. And so after making the thirty-five-mile trek to his place, I damn sure wasn't going for a few-mile putt—I would go to ride long every time. But first, I had to get the new bike there.

I had joined Cumberland County HOG* on buying the Sportster from the Millville, New Jersey, dealer. As a member, they invited me to their annual HOG Christmas party. It was at that party

---

* Harley Owners Group, the largest factory-sponsored riding organization in the world.

the Millville dealer told me, "If you buy a bigger bike from me, I'll give you what you paid for the Sportster."

I had been eyeing up the Springer at his shop since I bought the Sporty and responded immediately, "DEAL!"

We shook hands and sealed the fate of both bikes. Only problem was, Harley dealers close at year's end for as much as a few weeks into the New Year for inventory. I would have to wait to pick up the new bike for weeks. More than once during that time, I had flashbacks of anticipating my Sting-Ray. It felt much the same. Only then, I was thirty-one, not ten!

I had kept an eye on the weather leading up to the Friday night that Stacey agreed to drive me to the Millville dealership to pick up the new bike. I needed a ride because I had already dropped off the Sportster right after making the trade-in deal.

The temps during the entire week leading up to my pickup day had been in the teens and single digits, but the daytime high on the Friday pickup date was a tolerable thirty-five degrees. So while I knew it would be a chilly eighty-mile run back to Dad's garage, I figured it wouldn't be that bad. Wrong again!

By the time Stacey rolled us up to the front door of the dealer, the temperature had dipped back into the midtwenties. I was in for a cold solo ride all the way back to the old man's. Up to that point, I had never owned a bike with a windshield, including the new Springer. After all, being in the wind is what it was all about, right? I later put a detachable windshield on that Springer. That was like three layers of clothes up top, without the wind blowing directly on my upper body! It's incredible how much warmer a rider can be in winter with a windshield or fairing. Only that night, I would ride without one.

After completing the paperwork and receiving my keys, I put on my riding gear: leather biker jacket over a Windstopper sweater, leather chaps over jeans and wool long johns, a three-quarter helmet, and—most importantly—my lined leather gauntlet riding gloves.

Before we had gotten through Millville and into the dark farmlands of southern New Jersey, we encountered the first of four snow squalls that night. The wind blew the powdery snow right off the roads. I was suddenly thankful for the subfreezing temperatures all the preceding week because the ground was frozen and the snow didn't melt and slicken the roads on contact, which would have made for perfect conditions to dump a brand-new bike before even the first payment had been made.

Within only a few miles of the dealership, I was freezing. Despite having a zip-front leather jacket in contrast to the button front cloth coat I wore on that first freezing bicycle ride some twenty-one years earlier, the wind created from riding at fifty to seventy miles an hour finds its way past every zipper tooth to drill its way through any layers below to rob heat from your core. The worst, however, was my exposed chin and face. The three-quarter helmet did little to protect them. They were stinging badly by the time we got to Woodstown. I flagged Stacey down to follow me into their McDonald's at the edge of town so I could go in and warm up. And despite wearing leather gauntlets with Thinsulate insulation, my hands were *gone*!

I think my hands were toughened to cold weather from the frostbite I had gotten when I was ten. I sure as hell didn't want to repeat that episode but was concerned I might. It was damn cold out for riding without a windshield or fairing. Either would have deflected much of the wind from my hands.

We were forced back into the cold before I was ready because the McDonald's was about to close—nothing I could do but press on.

After my hands had been so cold for so long, they no longer hurt. That was the same order of events leading up to that horrible frostbite, and the thought of it gave me chills—of the other kind. Still, with no direct airflow over my gloved hands, the painless numbness didn't turn to waxy necrotic flesh that night and actually was a blessing in disguise—I no longer felt the painful cold discomfort. The worst was still ahead, however.

By the time we reached the Delaware Memorial Bridge, the fourth and final snow squall hit. The gusty wind blew me sideways, high above the three-mile-wide Delaware River somewhere in the inky blackness below. I struggled to keep the sleek black and chrome beauty in my lane, and again my chin and face were stinging badly.

At the tollbooth on the Delaware side, I couldn't feel my hands to get my wallet out, and the car drivers behind me were getting pissed off. But I had Stacey in her Z-24 as my "back door"—no worries!

At eighteen degrees, I had gotten to the point where I was asking myself if it were possible to feel any colder. I would get the answer in the next twenty-five miles or so to Odessa, where I once again flagged Stacey down to pull over—that time in the parking lot of the Hearth diner—so I could get into her car and warm up.

By then, I had gotten that gnawing hypothermic bone chill that takes hours to shake. In the car, I made a huge mistake—I took my gloves off and put my numb hands in front of the heater vents to bring them back to life. On reviving them, the stinging pain returned with a vengeance. I was miserable and still had about twelve more miles to go, which were the worst. Jeez, would I ever learn! I had made the mistake of running warm water over my hands that fateful Christmas night after getting frostbite; thawing them quickly in the car was no better.

By the time we rolled up to my father's house, the temperature had dropped to twelve degrees, and I was *done*! I could barely work the clutch and front brake. My face and chin were stinging horribly, and I was frozen through and through. But I made it—and in one piece too.

It took me hours once we got back to my apartment—with the thermostat maxed out—to recover from that cold. But I didn't care; I was the proud owner of a shiny new FXSTS and felt a similar euphoric high like I had felt on seeing that Kent Sting-Ray under the Christmas tree over two decades earlier.

On Saturday, I made the thirty-five-mile drive to my garaged bike and took it out all day in the relative heat wave at forty-two degrees. Only then, I stayed warm with the same clothes and riding gear I had worn the night before when it was thirty degrees colder.

That night, we visited Stacey's mom, who had just returned from visiting her boyfriend across the river in New Jersey. She had made the ride over the night before in that last snow squall. We realized we were on the bridge at the same time when she exclaimed, "Can you believe there was some nut riding a motorcycle in that snow and wind last night!"

Stacey and I looked at each other, and neither one of us had the heart to tell her mom that the nut she saw was her future son-in-law!

FIRST RIDES:
A HIDDEN CONNECTION

I suppose one reason I started riding motorcycles was because it pissed my father off to no end. He had what I viewed as an inordinate dislike of these inanimate machines, or "murdercycles" as he called them.

I'll never forget what happened one Saturday when I was seven while Dad had taken me and my brother to get our haircut at the same barber who had cut his hair when he was a kid. There was a city police motorcycle parked out in front of the barbershop, and I walked toward it to check it out.

I've always been deeply interested in mechanical things, even at that young age, so I was drawn to the machine instinctively, trying to understand how it worked. It was an early 1960s Harley-Davidson Panhead Duo Glide with foot clutch and tank shifter.

It didn't matter that I had no interest in riding the thing, but Dad practically yanked my arm from its socket while proclaiming, "As long as you live in my house, you'll *never* get on one of those!"

That was odd. I wondered what exactly I had done that might have deserved that outpouring. Twenty-five years later I would learn why.

Fast-forward to senior year in high school when my primary mode of transportation was my prized ten-speed bicycle.

My friend Mike's older brother, Chris, had joined the Marines and asked me and Mike to keep his 'Cuda and Harley running so that when he was home on leave, they'd both be ready to roll.

Mike had his own bike—a beautiful 1969 Triumph Bonneville—and he once asked me to ride Chris's bike with him. But I had never ridden and told him so.

"It's easy. I'll show you," Mike said. "Take Chris's 'Cuda and follow me over to the school parking lot."

I was a bit apprehensive and had no interest in riding a motorcycle anyway, but as an impressionable seventeen-year-old, no way would I admit that to Mike.

When we got to our school parking lot, Mike dismounted the bike—a 1977 Harley-Davidson FXE. The E stood for electric start. But the bike also had a fold-out kick-starter, which Mike instructed me to use to restart the bike. I pushed down on the starter until I felt resistance, like Mike told me to do. Then, while holding the throttle open a bit, I thrust the starter shaft down abruptly. The engine roared to life. The factory pipes back then delivered a satisfying syncopated rumble from the out-of-primary-balance V-twin 1,200 cc engine—a seventy-four-inch Harley. When I settled into the saddle, I could feel every detonation of the rigidly mounted engine through the frame. It felt alive, and I connected with it!

Next, Mike explained how to put the bike in gear and let out the clutch while simultaneously rolling on the throttle to get moving. I stalled the first two attempts but, on the third try, pulled away smoothly. And away I went—for about a hundred yards. I almost dumped the bike because I neglected to pull in the clutch while braking to get the big machine stopped.

Mike ran up and asked what was wrong. He had neglected to explain how to shift gears but covered that briefly for my next attempt.

I restarted the bike, no problem. I squeezed the clutch lever and found first gear, no problem. I managed to get up to third gear in the parking lot, no problem. But when I attempted to turn to avoid running off the asphalt into the grass, I didn't make it!

I dumped Chris's bike in the turf. At least I had bled off most of the forty miles an hour I had attained reaching third gear. I went down hard on my shoulder but was more worried about damage to the bike. Fortunately, there were only grass and mud scuffs down the right side—nothing serious.

Mike was laughing hysterically while yelling something to me about "counter steering," which I would soon learn is how a motorcycle above about twenty miles an hour is turned—that is, push right to go right, push left to go left. *You do not steer it like a bicycle*, which is what I had done wrong to wind up in the grass. Counter steering is necessary because the front wheel becomes a gyroscope while spinning.

Despite the less-than-stellar first ride, I was hooked! The vibration of that V-twin between the legs, the rumble of the exhaust, the wind in my hair *spoke* to me. And the best part was, Mike told me I could ride Chris's bike any time I wanted, and he gave me a key to their shed!

So for the rest of summer '78, I rode every chance I could get. I never took the bike home, however, lest I risk the old man finding out. I would ride my ten-speed bicycle the three miles to the shed, then get the Harley out and ride from there.

Later, I purposefully let the old man find out about my riding at a time when he and I just didn't see eye to eye on much at all. And I learned eventually why he had such a hard-on against "murdercycles."

Despite his aversion to motorcycles, Dad let me garage my 1992 Springer Softail at his house because I lived in an apartment back then and didn't want my bike unprotected on the street.

I was surprised to find Dad looking intently at my bike one day when I came over to take it for a ride.

Dad asked me, "What's this?" while pointing to the clutch lever and cable.

"The clutch."

After which he asked, "Then what's this?" while pointing to the shifter lever.

"That's the shifter, why?"

"Well, in my day, the clutch was here. And the shifter was on the gas tank, here."

I was dumbfounded that Dad knew *anything* about motorcycles, let alone the configuration of older tank-shift, foot-clutch machines.

But I could see he was interested in my bike, and that was gratifying. I coaxed him to tell me more because for so many years, my riding had been a source of silence between us.

Dad explained that his first ride was an unauthorized attempt at piloting a forty-five-inch WLA Harley from the motor pool on the army base where he was stationed back in the late 1940s.

I was stunned; I never knew he had ever ridden, even once.

Dad was friends with the sergeant in charge of the motor pool, who encouraged Dad to ride one of the Harleys. Those old bikes had foot clutches and three-speed tank shifters—arguably more challenging to ride than a modern hand-clutch, foot-shift machine.

Dad showed up at the motor pool barefoot when he was off duty one day, eager to ride a WLA. The sergeant instructed Dad how to start the engine and then engage first gear. Dad didn't go into the details of what he had done wrong—and likely didn't know—but he wrecked the bike. In doing so, he lost the skin on the tops of both feet.

Dad got reamed out, big-time, by his commanding officer for riding without authorization or proper training and for the damage done to Uncle Sam's property. But the greater price he paid was the painful months-long healing process from the severe road rash on his feet.

He said, "Everything happened so fast. I don't even know how the *tops* of my feet were injured, but I knew that was my last ride on a Harley."

I was fascinated. I too rode without proper training and even dumped the bike my first time in the saddle, but I wasn't seriously injured. Before buying the Springer, I had enrolled in an AMA motorcycle safety course to get lower insurance and to bypass the motor vehicle motorcycle riding test to get my license. It would be the first time I would have a license after fourteen years of riding without one. That course was an eye-opener. After taking it, I wondered how I had managed to keep from killing myself in those years before I received proper instruction in things like counter steering and low-speed clutch control!

I couldn't help but wonder, if Dad had not been injured and learned to ride properly, might he and I have shared my passion for riding? I would never know—he passed away before I ever had the chance to find out. But I was glad he told me that he once rode too.

Like father, like son…sort of!

Take That,
You DMV Prick!

Other than RUBs,* I've never met a biker who wasn't strapped for cash at one time or another. For some of us, we've even had to sell our prized Harley when finances were tight.

Aside from my 1940 EL Knucklehead that I would purchase many years later, my 1992 Softail Springer was the most visually striking bike that I ever owned. I had planned to keep that Springer forever.

Well, I had to sell that bike to keep a promise I had made to the old man. My wife Stacey and I bought our first house the year after I got the Springer. The following summer, I had planned to take the old man on a fly-in fishing trip for walleye and pike out of St. Ann du Lac, Canada. He was really looking forward to that trip. Only, I was strapped: new house, new furniture, new lawn mower, and the like. I wasn't gonna let the old man down, though.

The only quick source of cash I had was the equity in my bike mostly because I had been making double or triple payments on it before we got the house. The good news was that from the time I had bought it in '92 to '94, something phenomenal had happened. There were three or four buyers for every Harley the factory built, which made the resell market phenomenal too. That lasted until around 2004 or 2005 (after Harley's one hundredth anniversary hullabaloo died out).

---

* Rich Urban Bikers.

Anyway, the Springer sold easily, and I financed our fishing trip with money to spare. Despite feeling the gut-punch of being a biker without a bike, I delivered for the old man. It was worth it.

Not long after we got back from that fishing trip, I started looking for another bike. But what the hell! I was caught up in the era of excess demand in the face of too little supply. I should have realized that when I sold my Springer quickly and for a premium price. After that, I struggled to find *any* Harley to replace it. Screw me!

There were *no* new bikes to be had at any price. The dealers had waiting lists for everything scheduled to hit their floors. If I were to find a bike, it would have to come from another strapped-for-cash sorry ass like me.

Eventually I found an '89 FLST complete with Drag pipes. Those pipes were a might bit too loud for me to keep peace with my new neighbors, who already didn't like having "scooter trash" living next door. And while I had planned to redo the bike, including addition of baffled pipes, I needed to get the machine registered and inspected as is first.

One thing I hated when I lived in Delaware was they had this total government cluster fuck called the Division of Motor Vehicles, or just DMV. To get a vehicle tagged, it had to go through inspection first, even motorcycles. None of that bullshit at home here in Park County—I just go to the courthouse and pay my fees.

I knew I was in for a hard time when the low-wage jerk off working the floor at the inspection lanes yelled at me to bring the bike into the reinspection lane after I had been queued up in one of the normal lanes. There was no signage to indicate bikes went through the car reinspection lane only—how was I supposed to know?

That guy had a real hard-on against motorcycles—or bikers—apparently. The first thing he did was jam a bamboo stick into the pipes before bellowing out loud enough for everyone to hear: "FAILS! No baffles in them pipes!"

I never cracked the throttle on pulling up to the lanes, and the idle wasn't all that loud. Nevertheless, he immediately shoved that stick in the pipes before making his grand declaration. Then, he used the mirror on wheels—which is used to look under cars for holes in exhaust systems—to look under my bike. What the hell!

Just give me my failure slip and quit wasting my time! I thought.

When that prick was done, he handed me my slip and barked, "Use the *re*inspection lane when you come back after you get those loud pipes off that thing!"

Screw him! I wasn't going to change the pipes just to get the bike registered—no way. There were two solutions: wait until a brother I knew was working the lanes or buy the three-inch-long baffles that slide right up into the ends of the pipes before trying again. The bike had to be quieter on the next pass because the failure slip had on it in huge letters: "LOUD PIPES!" That really pissed me off because while that guy was wasting my time, a pickup truck in the inspection lane next to us passed even though it was obviously running glass-packs or cherry bomb mufflers! "Little Hitler" probably wasn't allowed to have a bicycle when he was a kid, so now he hates bikers. Whatever.

I went to the local Harley shop to get some baffles. They only had ones that required drilling the pipes and securing them with a short bolt, and only for two-inch pipes. The pipes on my bike were one and three-quarter inches.

So I went back to my garage to see what I could fabricate. I then remembered that the mufflers on my friend's old '70 Electra Glide were packed with fiberglass and could be tuned by adding or removing some packing. I didn't have much on hand in the garage; we hadn't been in the house very long. What I did find was some "000" steel wool. I figured I could stuff some of that just a few inches up into each pipe to drop the sharp crack to a dull rumble. That actually worked amazingly well—until I opened the throttle once I got on the main road out of the neighborhood. When I did, the "stuffing" blew out of both pipes, and the ear-splitting Drag pipe sound returned.

I circled back to the house. That time, I took the steel wool with me in the saddle bags and brought a wooden dowel along too. About a block from the DMV, I pulled over and restuffed the pipes. Only that time, I used the dowel to force the wool way inside the pipe, not just near the end as before. I made it to the reinspection lane just fine, although I think I used too much steel wool because the bike wasn't running well—it couldn't breathe right with the excessive wool choking the system.

As luck would have it, Little Hitler was still working the reinspection lane. I feathered the clutch and practically walked the bike up to the line so as not to blow the wool from the pipes. Because the bike was then *so* quiet, he never even jammed the stick in the pipes to feel for baffles.

I handed him my failure slip. He wouldn't even look me in the eye; he just handed me an "all-clear" slip. I was then good to go to get my tags.

All of a sudden it hit me: time to whack the throttle and clean the pipes, so to speak. Holy shit, I was unprepared for what happened next!

When I rolled the throttle on almost wide open, two *flaming* balls of steel wool shot from the pipes. Little Hitler had to jump out of the way! And off I went, with him screaming something as I left rubber in the inspection lane. I knew fine steel wool would burn, having set some on fire accidentally in metal shop back in high school, but man that shit is dangerous when ejected at high speed from a fire-breathing Harley!

I was *sure* Little Hitler ran inside to the waiting lines to try to put the brakes on my registration, but I decided not to go in. Instead, I headed home and returned the following week in the truck (inspection slips were good for thirty days).

I eventually redid that whole bike, including swapping out those ignorant-loud one-and-three-quarter-inch Drag pipes. But until I did, a smile would come over me every time I rode it—*legally tagged*—knowing that I had beaten Little Hitler in his DMV domain!

WHAT'S IN A NAME?

Back before Sturgis 2002, many bikers whom I would eventually meet during the rally had connected through a certain Sturgis online bulletin board. It was through that early social media vehicle that I met and befriended "Dave/Shovel/Max," or "Three-Name Dave" as I would refer to him. Dave was an interesting character, who had hand-built an amazing old-school chopper and who lived in the high desert of Washington state while at that same time, I was working and living in Delaware. So that bulletin board had succeeded in connecting bikers from across the country who had attended—or would attend, someday—the Sturgis Rally.

Dave/Shovel/Max was Three-Name Dave's online username on the bulletin board. Mine was EvlFukr, which stood for—you probably guessed it—Evil Fucker. That wasn't just some self-ascribed name I thought was cool or anything like that. It was a name I had *mistakenly* thought I had earned during a certain event that happened when I was thirty before I met my wife Stacey.

So anyway, I, Dave, and Scotty—another rider from the bulletin board—had concocted an idea to hold a run through the Black Hills of South Dakota on Monday of Sturgis Rally week. Among some of the other bulletin board members were locals of the town of Hill City, South Dakota, who persuaded the three of us to start the run at the Mangy Moose Saloon that was, at that time, on the main drag in Hill City. We three didn't care because none of us were locals anyway and were each coming from completely different parts of the country—Dave from Washington, Scotty from Colorado, and me from Delaware.

After much back-and-forth about what to name the run, we settled eventually on the First Annual Mangy Moose Monday Run

(MMM). Okay, so perhaps it was a bit presumptive to think that the run would be anything other than a one-time get-together among members of that Sturgis online bulletin board. Nevertheless, that run was repeated during Sturgis for many years after that and even after the Mangy Moose Saloon was forced to reopen in an alternate location because the original building's owner refused to extend the original bar's lease.

Anyway, Mangy Moose Monday was on for Sturgis 2002. We board members all had a reasonably good idea of what one another looked like from the various pictures each of us had uploaded in many of our online posts. So it was easy for me to identify Scotty on the sidewalk outside the Mangy Moose after I rolled into Hill City and parked my Wide Glide in front of the bar. We went into the bar to wait for Dave, who was late per our agreed-to rallying time. While waiting in the bar, Casey and his wife arrived from Big Timber, Montana; Georgia Julie from Atlanta; Road King Carl; and even a couple of riders from Canada who had joined the board to participate in the MMM had arrived, along with countless others from across the country. Noon was approaching, and the Mangy Moose was getting packed with lunch patrons who weren't privy to the MMM run.

We were all getting eager to roll, but Dave hadn't shown up yet. Dave was sort of the unofficial "chairman of the board," having gained the respect of most members because he was naturally like-able—a trait that came through in his posts—and because of the homemade chopper that he had fabricated and used for his everyday rider. Also, Dave was one of the three of us who were the designated co-road captains for the run; we weren't leaving without him.

By and by, Dave came through the front door. He spied me across the crowded bar and immediately hollered out, "Evil Fucker!" with his arms outstretched as he headed my way. The place almost went silent!

I didn't know whether to die of embarrassment or bust out laughing while the patrons appeared to be wondering what the hell was unfolding before them. I busted up laughing as I embraced Dave; it was the first time we met in person. After we slapped each other on the back, the stunned crowd went back to doing whatever they had been doing before Dave made his grand entrance and christened me, Evil Fucker, for the entire bar to hear. The name hadn't gone unnoticed by some of the MMM riders, who asked me what it meant. I had no intention of going into *that* story, and certainly not then.

Scotty and I busted Dave's balls for being late. Dave claimed that he had a hard time finding parking. While parking during any rally can be hit or miss, riders are coming and going all the time. So usually going around the block a time or two will score you a slot big enough to back your tire to the curb. That's why Scotty and I just smirked at Dave's excuse—until we went outside and saw, for the first time, Dave's chopper and enormous trailer that he had hand-fabricated. It turned out that all Dave had to do was double- or triple-park the long bike and trailer in front of other bikes! That was the first time I saw Dave's creation and the crowds that it drew.

On seeing Dave's machine, Scotty and I realized that Dave had straight up told the truth about having trouble finding a parking place!

Then, despite being well past our target kick-stands-up time, we returned to the Moose to socialize a while longer so that we all could get to know many familiar board members in the flesh. While many knew of one or a few other members, we all new Dave through his many helpful Harley technical posts and the amusing biker stories he shared. He inspired certain board members into taking long road trips for their first time, including several members who rode long to make the MMM run.

Dave holding court before we finally kicked off the first MMM run.

I can't recall the exact route that we took through the Hills that day, but we stopped periodically for group photos and to let certain riders catch up. Dave, Scotty, and I flogged the throttle through all the tight turns in Custer State Park, and some riders couldn't keep our brisk pace.

The three co-road captains for that first MMM run while stopped at Custer State Park. From left to right are Scotty on his wishbone-framed Shovelhead chopper, Dave on his long bike Shovelhead chopper, and the author on his '99 Harley Dyna Wide Glide.

That was a memorable get-together. After the run, many of us stopped at a campground, where many of the board members were staying, to continue the party and shoot the shit a while longer around a huge campfire.

That's where Georgia Julie asked Dave what "Dave/Shovel/Max" meant. I was curious too and listened in.

Julie asked, "So, Dave, what do the three names mean in your board name? I mean, Dave is pretty obvious, but what about Shovel and Max?"

Dave replied, "Shovel is short for the type of Harley motor that powers my bike—a Shovelhead. Max is just another name some of my close friends call me."

Dave excused himself to mingle with other board members around the campfire, and as he got up to leave, Brett joined us.

Julie then turned to me and asked, "Jay, where did EvlFukr come from? You seem pretty nice to me."

Shit! I wasn't prepared to explain that and dodged her question. Then Brett joined in on prying for the answer because he had also asked me back at the Moose what my board name meant. Because they made such a big deal of it, I finally laid out the backstory.

I began, "One early summer evening many years ago, I was walking in the local park down by the waterfront. I noticed this really attractive young girl sitting by herself on one of the benches. The park has this mile-and-a-half asphalt pathway that follows the shoreline of the river, and I would usually take that path from end to end a few times on each walk. On my second pass, there was an equally attractive older woman sitting with the girl I had seen on my first time around. The woman looked up as I was nearing their bench and smiled, so I said hi. She responded, 'Why don't you join us? It's too hot and humid for walking.'

"It really was, and I didn't want to get sweaty anyway because I was headed out to the bars after the park. It was a Saturday night. The woman and I chatted for a few minutes. Her name was Kathryn. After a while, she turned my attention to the young girl who was seated on the other end of the bench before saying to me, 'You seem really nice. I think you would make a good match for my daughter, Kaitlin, over there.'

"Before I could respond, the young girl said, 'Mom! You're embarrassing me!' I could see the resemblance—Kaitlin was clearly a younger version of her still-hot mom. Anyway, it was awkward. Here's this hot mom sort of pimping her very attractive daughter to me. It was weird—"

Julie broke in, "And…what did you do…?" in a rather accusing voice.

"Nothing…that night. But I did get Kaitlin's phone number— from her mom—which was also her number because Kaitlin still lived at home. I wound up dating Kaitlin, despite the ten-year age difference between us—I was thirty. She was just twenty—and with her mom's total approval. I later learned that Kathryn was only forty-two and—"

Brett interrupted, "Uh-oh, this is sounding like the start of a Penthouse Forum story," before he started laughing.

"You have no idea, Brett!"

Then Julie perked up, "What has this got to do with your board name, EvlFukr?"

I continued, "After dating for a couple of months, I was told I must meet Kaitlin's father. He had insisted. Turns out, Kathryn was divorced, and even though her daughter was over eighteen, Dad insisted he meet whoever was seeing his daughter. Fair enough, I thought.

"When Dad came over, I about shit my pants! He was a cop I had had a run-in with when I was twenty-two while I was doing some one-percenter shit back when I was a hang-around with a local club, hoping to get prospected. Anyway, let's just say that that meeting was tense! I was suddenly totally immersed in dating his daughter and wanted to let him know in the worst way that I was banging daddy's little girl!"

Julie spoke up, "Well *that's* pretty evil!" before she joined Brett laughing.

"You ain't heard the half of it, Julie."

"Well, go on…"

"As summer went on, I would have sex with Kaitlin all over her mom's house. I was sure her mom heard us a few times before she eventually walked in on us once. I expected her to read me the riot act, but she didn't say anything. She also didn't leave or close the door immediately—she just stared for a moment while I was pile-driving her daughter! *That* was weird!"

"Holy shit!" Julie said. She then propped herself up on one elbow, listening more intently than she had been up to that point.

"The next couple of times I came over to hang out or just pick up Kaitlin, her mom would sit on the couch real close to me on one side while Kaitlin was on the other. Also, Kathryn had started wearing really provocative blouses and without a bra. As hot and built as Kaitlin was, her mom outshined her physically. She had massive tight breasts, a tiny waist, and a full round ass and hips. I got a hard-on a couple of times when Kathryn came in the room. I only hoped Kaitlin wouldn't notice or, if she did, think it was because of her. I didn't really think anything of her mom's behavior because after all, I thought I was just being full of myself, thinking that this hot forty-two-year-old was attracted to me, a thirty-year-old boyfriend of her own flesh-and-blood daughter. I admit, I did fantasize about getting it on with Kathryn, but I had never cheated on a steady girlfriend and wasn't about to blow the good thing I had with Kaitlin if by some miracle, an opportunity with Kathryn happened along."

Julie jumped in, "You didn't…did you?"

"Well, uh, let me explain…"

"Jay! You *did*, didn't you!" And with that, Julie roared laughing.

I went on, "So one day, I got a call from Kathryn. She invited me over to help her plan Kaitlin's twenty-first birthday party. She said Kaitlin was out and wouldn't return for several hours, which I already knew because Kaitlin had told me she was going out with her girlfriend Vicky before visiting her father afterward.

"I went over, and Kathryn had been drinking. She wasn't drunk but noticeably relaxed. She was wearing a heavy terry cloth bath robe, which kind of freaked me out, I have to admit. She offered me a beer, and I accepted. We sat there on the couch, each sipping our beer from the bottle for a few awkward silent minutes. Out of the blue,

Kathryn puts her leg up over my legs, without saying a word. I got an instant hard-on! When I glanced over at her, she was mouthing the neck of that bottle like she was giving head! I didn't say a word—I was stunned."

Julie said, "Oh my god, she wanted your horny ass!"

"Horny is right! My cock was throbbing! I still didn't act on my urge though because—in my twisted mind—I was wondering whether that was some sick test to check my loyalty to Kaitlin."

Through steady laughter, Julie asked, "So how'd you do?"

"Oh, I failed miserably!"

"I knew it! I knew it!" Julie repeated. "You *are* an evil fucker!"

"Well, not quite yet I wasn't. After Kathryn rubbed my rock-hard cock through my jeans with her foot, I was done. I surrendered to pure lust—and so did she. I stripped before practically ripping her robe from her. And we did everything imaginable between two consenting adults, right there on the couch, the coffee table, and the living room floor. It was the most intense sex I had experienced up to that time and was probably better still because she was forbidden fruit—the mother of my hot girlfriend."

"Evil fucker! Evil fucker! Evil fucker!" Julie kept repeating while laughing uncontrollably.

"Not quite yet, Julie, but that was coming soon enough. While I had her knees up around her head and was working on getting my third nut, the front door opened! In came Kaitlin and her dad—Kathryn's ex-husband, the cop—but only long enough for Kaitlin to yell out, 'You EVIL FUCKER!' before her dad yanked her back out the door.

"At that moment, I didn't care. I was hell-bent on finishing off Kathryn who was writhing fiercely and who—apparently—didn't care either. She didn't miss a beat!"

"Oh…my…god!" Julie uttered while shaking her head at me.

"Hey, don't judge me—I was seduced!" was my excuse. But Julie wasn't buying it—that is, until I told her the rest of the story.

"I figured there was no coming back from that infidelity. My relationship with Kaitlin would, no doubt, be over and done with. I was right. I felt really guilty about it and tried to contact Kaitlin, but it was difficult. I couldn't call her, else risk her mom picking up. I tried to go through her friend Vicky, and when I explained to her what had happened, she unloaded on me with a real eye-opener.

"Vicky told me, 'Kaitlin wasn't screaming at you. She was screaming at her mother.' Vicky went on to tell me that I was Kaitlin's fifth boyfriend that her mom had seduced!"

Julie perked up, "*Are you shitting me!*"

"Nope. Kathryn had procured Kaitlin's five most recent boyfriends, much like she had done with me at the park, only to later bag them herself. So you see, *I* wasn't really an evil fucker after all—Kathryn was! And besides, what's in a name, anyway!"

"Well, okay," Julie said. "But that just means *you're a pig*! Ha ha ha!"

"Ha ha! I can live with that…"

Soon after getting home from Sturgis that year, I changed by bulletin board username to TwistAWrist. That name required no explanation among bikers!

DAVE'S LONG BIKE
BEATS 'EM ALL!

As I have traveled the country on my Harleys, I have met some of the most interesting bikers and have seen the custom motorcycles they have built that reflect their fabrication skills and are an expression of their individuality. My friend Dave is one such rider, who created one of the most unique pieces of rolling Americana I have ever seen.

As crudely manufactured as Dave's long bike had been, it is a legitimate piece of American folk art, purpose built using whatever salvaged parts he could find; what he couldn't find, he fabricated. And while most riders might think it is a death trap because of the suicide clutch and open belt primary that could snag your pants in the drive sprockets, it is actually a great ride, and it pulls strong with the over-sized Shovelhead motor stuffed into that rigid frame. It is an example of American ingenuity that spawned a form-follows-function bare bones functional machine worthy of awards. Case in point: the reason Dave was late meeting me the day we were leaving Sturgis to head up into Montana to visit another biker friend of ours.

I was set to meet Dave at the entrance of his campground. We would head out together from there, across Wyoming and up into Big Timber, Montana, where Casey lived. We wanted to hit the road early enough so we could make it to Casey's with plenty of daylight to spare so we could socialize awhile before we had to roll out the next morning.

Dave was late again. I didn't sweat it because I figured that with all the stuff he had to pack into that monstrous trailer, he was just running behind. After an hour though, I began to wonder whether he had ever made it back the night before from the Dungeon Bar or the Full Throttle Saloon, two places we frequented while at the rally.

Back in '03, I got my first cell phone—a huge thing with a holster that was nearly as big as the holster for my Colt 1911A1 .45 pistol that I carried back then. Cell service was spotty everywhere in that part of South Dakota and farther west, and battery life was short. So I usually only turned the phone on to make a call or check for messages, and then turned it right back off again. Dave also had one of those early cell phones, so I checked to see whether he had called while I was threading my way down from Keystone, up in the Hills, where I preferred to camp because I don't like the heat down in the rally campgrounds just outside of Sturgis. Sure enough, Dave had called and left a message. It was difficult to understand over the background noise, but I heard something about "...All the beer I could drink..." and "...Kicking ass on all those trailer queens..." which meant nothing to me. The only useful part I got was that he would be back at the campground by 11:00 a.m.—fully two hours after we had planned to roll out.

Well, that was a relief. He hadn't run into any trouble at the Dungeon or Full Throttle and would be along soon. I kicked back and slung my boots over the handlebars of my Wide Glide and sunned myself in the warm morning South Dakota sunshine while waiting for Dave to return.

Before long, I heard the unmistakable note from his hand-fabricated two-into-one exhaust. I looked up, and there came Dave with a shit-eating grin on his face. I dismounted my "sun chair" and walked over toward him.

As I approached, he yelled, "Hey, check this out!" as he simultaneously flipped back the lid on the trailer. After digging around a bit, he withdrew a sizable trophy.

I asked, "What's that for?"

"First place in the ride-in bike show!" he exclaimed with that grin still on his face.

"What!"

"Yeah, this morning I'm sitting here on the bike, minding my business, when two guys with name tags on their shirts and one carrying a clipboard walk up and ask me if I'd be interested in entering my bike in the annual Sturgis Rally ride-in bike show. I tell 'em I'm sitting right here waiting on a friend to meet me, but they were insistent that my bike should be seen in the show. I asked them how long it would take and if it would be okay if I parked the bike in the show and then walked back here to join you. The guy with the clipboard tells me, 'Entrants must be present to win and have to stay on the show grounds with their ride.' I wasn't gonna budge, but then the other guy tells me, 'You can have all the beer you want for free.' Well, Jay, I knew you wouldn't mind if I took him up on that offer, so I entered the bike."

"Are you friggin' kidding me!" I said. "And you won *first place?*"

"Yes, sir, mister. And I couldn't believe it because out the back of these high-dollar tractor-trailers, one after another, I see bikes from Jesse James, Billy Lane, and Indian Larry—all the top builders. And all them bikes were shiny show-room clean trailer queens—never been ridden, other than to ride into the show. I figured I got *no* shot up against all that custom shit. So I spent the time going back and forth, one beer at a time, filling my Igloo with the free beer they offered me."

At that point, I was laughing so hard at Dave's one-beer-at-a-time cooler run that it was hard to pay attention. But I listened as he went on.

"So, Jay, you would have loved it. I *knew* I was going to win at one point."

"Dave, how could you *know* for sure before they announced the winner?"

"Because I overheard the judges talking," Dave replied.

"And…what *exactly* did they say?"

"Well, two of them were trying to convince another one that my bike should win. They said, 'Look at this thing, man, it's hand built, and it was actually ridden here from Washington. You can see all the road grime and bugs. This son of a bitch is a rider, not like those thirty- and forty-thousand dollar prissy trailer queens!' Finally, the third guy agreed, and at that point, I knew it was in the bag."

"Holy shit, Dave, that's incredible. Congratulations!"

And with that, he stowed the trophy back into the trailer, and we left Sturgis '03 on our way to Big Timber, Montana, and big fun at Casey's.

Everywhere we stopped for gas or for the night for the rest of that trip, Dave's bike would draw a crowd. It was appreciated for its uniqueness by more than just bikers. After all, it is a piece of rolling artwork. Dave still rides that same bike today.

DAVE STRIKES OUT
FOR LOS ANGELES

My friend Dave was an electrician at the Hanford Nuclear Facility in Washington state where the uranium for the bombs Fat Man and Little Boy had been enriched during WWII and subsequently unleashed on Hiroshima and Nagasaki. Hanford had been in cleanup mode since the 1970s, and each time a new company won the contract for the ongoing decontamination, all the same workers were rehired but at reduced pay or benefits, or both. Dave had had enough of watching his seniority grow while his salary declined, so he sought work in California.

In spring of 2004, Dave packed all that he could carry on his hand-built chopper and headed to Los Angeles to begin work as a lineman. He had been a foreman at Hanford, but he was willing to start over in LA for better pay and benefits and—perhaps for the real reason—to become part of the Southern California motorcycling scene.

I talked with Dave before he struck out toward a completely new life in LA. He left his house to his ex-wife, his pickup truck to his son, and only took the chopper as his sole means of transportation, loaded with only the most essential personal possessions, like his tools, clothes, and a $500 pair of White's and Hathorn lineman's boots.

I had done work in the Bay Area and knew quite well how expensive it was to live anywhere along the coast, so I asked him where he was going to live. I'll never forget that conversation.

"Dave, where did you find a place to live in LA?"

"Oh, I don't have a place yet. I'll find something when I get there."

"What! You're gonna ride your chopper to LA to start a new job and you don't even have a place to live yet? You're friggin' nuts!"

"Aw, you know me, Jay. I won't be living under the boardwalk for more than a week before I find a place, and besides, I don't know which shop I'll be assigned to. So no sense in finding a place until I know where I'll be working. I want to be as close to the shop as possible."

"WHAT! You mean you took this job without knowing where you'll be assigned? As the low man in the pecking order, you could wind up being assigned to East LA in the middle of the gang bangers!"

"Aw, that doesn't bother me. You know I make friends easy."

That was absolutely true. Dave could get along with almost anyone in a couple of minutes talking or less. If anyone could pick up his life and relocate to take a new job without knowing the exact assignment or having a place to live and pull it off, Dave could do it. And I'm here to tell you that he landed on his feet and in style too. Some people have a guardian angel, and Dave is one of them.

As luck would have it, despite Dave being the new guy, he pulled a cherry assignment working right out of the Hollywood main shop because his new employer recognized Dave's former foreman experience and wanted to groom him to lead in a future role. On his second day of work, his boss told him about a place to live right smack in the center of Beverly Hills within walking distance of Wilshire Boulevard and Rodeo Drive!

I remember Dave telling me that as I hung on every word in disbelief.

"Beverly Hills! Dave, I know you're making great money, but can you afford to live in *Beverly Hills*?"

"Yes, sir, mister, a thousand bucks a month."

"What! That's dirt cheap for an apartment in the heart of Beverley Hills. How can the rent be so cheap?"

"Well, this here hotel used to be one of the finer ones back in the day [Dave was living at the Beverly Hills Reeves Hotel, or just The Reeves]. Over time, the area got built up, and all the land around the hotel was swallowed up. Now, no one wants to stay here because there's no parking. All the newer hotels and offices have parking garages, like the Rolex building next door. So the Reeves still rents some rooms nightly but most rooms, like mine, are now efficiency apartments. Rent stays low because the apartment renters constantly spend time moving their cars on the street because the parking is for one hour only until after 6:00 p.m. So most efficiency apartment renters don't stay long after they rack up dozens of parking violations.

"I don't have that problem because the manager lets me keep my bike right out in the alley next to the rear entrance. Cars can't fit past the bollards, but the bike slips on by. Plus, I have a barbecue grill set up out back and cook most meals outside. And the best part is, because this is still a hotel, housekeeping cleans and makes up my room, the same as a nightly rental."

"You lucky bastard!" was all I could spit out.

Dave just chuckled. He knew he had scored an incredible job and living quarters too. We continued our talk and made plans for me to come visit him on my summer run.

While my wife Stacey and I ran our business, we worked six to seven days a week, ten to fourteen hours a day, but when we played, we went big. We would block our calendars well ahead of any time off and let our clients know how to reach us and delegate most business decisions to trusted employees. That is how I was able to take five- to six-week long summer road trips in the saddle of my Harleys for many years.

In July 2004, I set out to ride what's left of Route 66 on my '04 Road King. And so I rode to nearly the start of the "Mother Road" in Chicago and headed west. That was one memorable ride, but some of the best of that run was spent with Dave once I got to LA.

We had agreed that when I got close—a relative term while on a motorcycle road trip—I would call Dave for final directions to his place. So the day I headed out from Albuquerque, New Mexico, I called Dave to finalize plans. That's when I discovered how expensive a room for one night in Beverly Hills was going to cost me.

The cheapest room I could find was $450 per night! For that much money in the heart of America, I could get seven to eight nights in mom-and-pop motels off the interstate. And that price was if I could score a vacancy. I called Dave back and asked if he could recommend any hotels or motels farther out from downtown Beverly Hills.

"Hell, man, just stay at my place," Dave said.

"Are you sure? That's a generous offer, and I wouldn't want to put you out."

"Yes, sir, mister, you're always welcome at my place."

"I'll tell you what. I'll buy dinner in exchange for my free room. Sound good?"

"Sure, if you want."

"Have you ever heard of Spago?"

"Can't say I have, Jay. What's that?"

"Well, I don't know either, but I heard it's where a lot of Hollywood players eat. And the food is supposed to be top shelf. It's somewhere in Beverly Hills. I'll call for reservations."

"Thanks, Jay!"

It was three easy days' riding from Albuquerque to LA, with plenty of Route 66 tourist time. The day after I talked to Dave, I got a message he had left on my cell phone. He was concerned about my offer to pay for dinner at Spago. He had told the guys on his crew, and they warned him how expensive it would be. He didn't want me getting blindsided with a huge dinner bill.

Nevertheless, I didn't call him back or cancel the reservation. I mean, really, if dinner cost me under $450, I was still ahead on account of the free room Dave was providing. And anyway, a deal's a deal.

It was brutally hot coming in across the Mojave Desert, and I didn't want another day in the saddle like that. When I called Dave from my room in Barstow, California, at ten o'clock at night, it was still 102 degrees. He told me I was only two hours from the Hooters on Santa Monica Boulevard, where he was sipping beers in the cool 72 degree ocean breeze and to roll on in. It was tempting, but I didn't want to miss any of 66 riding at night. So I told him I would see him by noon the next day.

I rolled out the next morning, eager to connect with Dave. To sum it up, Dave is the person from whom I stole the expression, "There's always more fun to be had!" Dave—like my other friends

Gabby and Paul—could always be counted on for a good time and in the most unlikely situations. I mean, really, anyone who could build a radical chopper like his and use that for his everyday ride in LA traffic has got to have a sense of humor!

I was equally eager to get off the Mojave Desert and leave the heat behind. Everything was going well until I got on the I-10, where all lanes came to a halt. I noticed other bikers splitting lanes, and so I began to follow them. To my amazement, the cagers were aware of us and would go wide in both lanes that we were splitting—*Pretty cool!* I thought. That saved me a lot of time and kept the Road King's air-cooled V-twin from overheating.

Once I arrived in Beverly Hills, I called Dave from Rodeo Drive to get final directions. Much to my surprise, Dave really was right downtown. I followed his directions down Wilshire Boulevard. Where I was to make my last turn, there he stood on the corner, waving me in—like the ground crew at an airport—right up the alley behind the Reeves where he parked his chopper.

I parked next to Dave's bike and private barbecue pit. Only in Cali could a modest country boy from the high desert in Washington end up in the heart of Beverly Hills set up like this:

"Hey, you crazy son of a bitch!" was the first thing out of Dave's mouth. And so that was my official welcome to Beverly Hills.

Since I had seen his bike last, I noticed a few changes—a "new" gas tank (well, new to his machine) and an early Evo-era primary cover.

"What's with that?" I asked, pointing to the primary cover, where previously an open belt drive had been visible.

"Well, she still has the kick starter, but if I stall in the traffic around here, I wanted electric legs to quickly get her going again. So I added an inner and outer primary from an early Softail with the starter mounted on top. Because she wasn't wired for a starter from the handlebars, I took this piece of hacksaw blade and mounted it here next to the solenoid so I could slide my heel over to push it in to contact the lead and crank the motor over. Works pretty nice!"

"Damn, Dave, now that you're making big bucks here in LA, why don't you just buy a new Twin Cam?"

You'd a thought I farted in church by the look on his face.

"I'll never get rid of this bike, mister. I built her from the ground up."

I understood—completely. "You ready for dinner?" I asked.

"Sure, let's get your stuff upstairs, then we'll go find Spago."

Dave helped me unpack my bike and carry all my gear up to his apartment. Then he gave me the nickel tour of the Reeves. Besides his private parking lot and barbecue pit, Dave also spent a lot of time up on the roof, where he also had a lounge chair and cooler. From top to bottom, Dave had become the king of the Reeves! I would have expected nothing less from him.

Dave got directions to Spago from the guy on the front desk, and we mounted up and rolled out into heavy traffic. I thought it was amusing that while Dave and his bike got stares everywhere we went the summer before all over the West, he barely got a sideways glance in Beverly Hills. I guess Dave and his ride were just not that unusual for So Cal.

I cracked up when we rolled up to Spago. It was literally closer and easier to walk to from the Reeves than take the one-way streets to ride to it. Dave had no idea that he lived that close to one of the area's celebrity magnets.

Then the fun began. There was valet parking only, and the black-and-white suited valets had no idea how to ride our bikes to the off-site parking lot. They very sheepishly asked us to follow one of the valet-driven cars to the parking lot from where they would bring us back in someone's car.

The very next car that had to return to the restaurant was a silver Rolls Royce V-12 Phantom. The parking lot valet sprinted over and opened the back door for us, like it was a limo. I looked at Dave, and he looked at me as we both started to crack up as we climbed in the back of someone else's high-end ride.

When we arrived back at Spago, another valet opened the door for us. As we climbed out from the back seat of the Phantom, we overheard people in the very long line to get in whispering things like, "Who's *that*!" and "Who are *they*!"

Dave and I were busting at the seams. We "obviously" were some high-dollar celebrities, as far as the uninformed crowd knew. The doorman, who already knew we had reservations, only added to our pseudo celebrity mystique by escorting us up to the front door ahead of those in line.

Once inside, Dave was like a kid in a candy store, starstruck on pointing out different TV and movie actors, none of whom I recognized except Tom Cruise. And just like any other patrons, we were seated in among the Hollywood elite, clad in our dirty road clothes while others around us were dressed in anything from jeans and t-shirts to three-piece Vanquish suits that cost more than my bike and Dave's combined.

I said, "Hey, Dave, you have *arrived*!"

"Holy shit! I didn't know *this* place was here."

We ordered our meals, and then reminisced about past runs to Sturgis, Daytona, Laconia, Laughlin—all the big rallies.

Dave then asked me, "So how was the ride out?"

"Great. Weather was good, and I did most of the old Route 66. It's a real pain in the ass in Texas though because you jump off the Super Slab [I-40] on seeing the Historic Route 66 signs. You then go through some small town that died when the Super Slab bypassed it back in the seventies, and then the road literally ends and turns to broken-up asphalt and grass. You have to double back and jump back on the Super Slab. I skipped a few of these sections because there was no real continuity anyway. The best most-preserved part is in Arizona. I only lost the road coming in over the El Cajon pass."

"How was traffic?"

"No problems with traffic until I got almost here, out on the I-10—it was a parking lot. But I joined some other bikers who were splitting lanes, so it wasn't that bad. I was impressed at how courteous the cagers were—"

"Courteous!" Dave interrupted. "They weren't being courteous, Jay. They were just worried about you scratching their Bentleys and Mercedes! And out here, mister, bikers and pedestrians are protected species. I couldn't believe all the questions on the California driver license exam about pedestrians and motorcycle rider rights. It's a riders' paradise—well, that is, until you come across a pesky pedestrian at some crosswalk!"

"Paradise, eh? Well, I'll take the weather anytime. But it's too crowded for me, Dave, but I hear the restaurants aren't bad."

"Yeah, you mean like *this* one?"

"Well, I don't know for sure, but we're about to find out. Here he comes…"

The waiter brought the first of seven fantastic courses. The food at Spago was everything the five-star ratings made it out to be. We finished off with some to-die-for chocolate dessert, whose name I don't recall, and great coffee. I remember telling Dave while on the phone from Albuquerque not to worry about the price because he saved me $450 on hotel room fees by putting me up at his place. Well, there was a net savings after paying the bill—$340 tab plus tip—so you could argue I was $110 ahead. That was the single most expensive meal for two I had ever eaten up to that time. But let me tell you, it was worth it—for the food and the free entertainment, just watching Dave gawk in awe at some of his TV heroes, and the crowd's reaction on our arrival in a Rolls Phantom and then again on being shuttled back to our bikes in a Bentley Continental GT before the long two-block ride back to the Reeves.

Dave and I laughed about our celebrity status for years afterward—all because the valets couldn't ride a Harley—and it was all at the expense of some unknown Rolls and Bentley owners. Not bad for a couple of working stiffs on holiday!

We turned in as soon as we got back to the Reeves. The next day was going to be a fun run up the coast to a number of celebrity biker hangouts that Dave had discovered in the short time since he had arrived in Cali, like the Rock Store up on Mulholland Highway, where Dave had schooled Jay Leno on the features of his chopper.

And I knew that riding with Dave, "There's always more fun to be had!"

BOXER BREAK

In a bar in Utah back in '07, I shattered the left orbit of a guy who assaulted me and, in so doing, gave myself a "boxer break" to the right hand. (Actually, I was in a "club." Until the 2008 Olympics were hosted in Utah, there were no "bars"—the Mormons controlled drinking in the state, or so I was told. However, you could go to a club—aka a *bar*—and become a member on the spot. You would register with the bartender, who had to record everything you drank! Since then, the laws were changed to accommodate the Olympics. Now those old blue laws are history.)

I was on the road that day on my '05 Harley Electra Glide headed to Grand Canyon from Cody, Wyoming. I stopped in Roosevelt, Utah, to grab a burger and a beer before checking into my motel for the night. I was in my riding leathers and traveling solo. I went in and registered with the bartender and made some small talk with her after ordering my dinner.

While I was sitting there minding my own business, some half-drunk asshole came up to me and started yelling, "Look at the tough biker dude," while getting in my face.

So I got up from the bar, grabbed my beer, and moved to a table. He went back to his table with his half dozen equally intoxicated buddies, calling me a "pussy."

I shot back, "You are what you eat!"

On hearing that, his friends and the bartender busted up laughing. That made him mad. Less than a minute went by, and he came over to my table yelling his "tough pussy biker" comments again. So again, I grabbed my beer and moved—that time, back to the bar, right in front of the bartender—in case I needed a witness. And again he went back to his table, but then his buddies were egging

53

him on. Sure enough, he came walking back toward me, and as he did, I watched him in the bar back mirror. Only that time, he put his hand on my shoulder and tried to spin me around on my stool—or possibly coldcock me. You never know in a situation like that. I was ready for him. I whirled around, and with all of my might, I buried my clenched right fist squarely in his face. I followed through on the punch as though his face had been three feet farther back than it was. Well, he hit his head on the bar, and then crumpled up on the floor in convulsions.

I'm screwed now! I thought.

In these small Utah towns, it seems everyone is related to everyone else and one of their relatives is often the local sheriff. I figured I would be headed to jail that night, and that son of a bitch would die right there on the floor in front of me while his goons would rat pack me for sure. But they were stunned; not one of them moved, not even to come to their friend's aid. I just sat back down and kept my eyes on them.

The bartender called the sheriff and said to me, "You'd better stay put!"

In the meantime, my food arrived at the bar, and I had my last dinner as a free man for a while. Or so I imagined...

Within minutes, the biggest cop I have ever seen in my life came through the front door. He was almost seven feet tall and seemed about four feet wide—no shit! He had to duck coming in the door with his hat on. That guy must have been raised on USDA-approved hormone-rich Utah beef. Even money says his mother had died in child birth—the guy was huge!

The officer spoke to the bartender for a minute, and on hearing what she told the giant cop, I rejoiced. I had once read that state prosecutors and judges all understand that eyewitness testimony is the least reliable. They all prefer forensic evidence because people just don't get the details right. And just then, I learned why.

I heard the bartender say to the cop, "He [the out-cold mess on the floor] hit him [me] first."

Not true, exactly, but definitely in my favor. The guy grabbed me, as a sloppy drunk is prone to do, but he didn't actually "hit" me.

I anticipated that he was going to do that very thing and was justified in my actions, but still, I threw the first punch—and last and only one as it turned out. I knew to keep my mouth shut and not clarify the bartender's statement.

Shortly after the officer entered the bar, paramedics came in. I got up from my stool to get out of the way, and as I did, Gigantor barked, "Sɪᴛ! Hᴇʀᴇ!" pointing to the table closest to the door but out of the way. I didn't need to be told twice by a peace officer, and certainly not by *that* one!

I overheard the paramedics, who raced to give aid on learning the guy had been convulsing, say something about a likely shattered something-or-other. I assumed he cracked his skull on falling backward and was in bad shape—possibly in critical condition.

All the while as that was unfolding, my heart was beating out of my chest.

I thought, *Screw him! What about me? I'm the victim here!*

Once the paramedics rolled the guy out on a stretcher and secured him for the ride to the local emergency room, the officer sat down next to me and asked me what happened.

I told him, "I stopped in for dinner after a long day on the road. I was minding my business. And that guy started in on me about being a 'pussy biker,' and I moved twice to avoid a problem. And then—"

Gigantor interrupted, "Why didn't you just leave?"

That *really* pissed me off, as though it were my responsibility to give up my freedom for some asshole.

So—as calmly as I could—I went on, "I had already ordered and paid for my meal, and besides, this is the only place around to grab a hot meal before turning in for the night." I added, "That parking lot is full of pickups, and what if that guy thought it would be fun to follow me and possibly run me off the road? There's no such thing as a fender-bender on a bike. For my safety, this had to end here."

The officer nodded acknowledgment, and then asked, "Did he hit you first?"

Without missing a beat, I said, "Yes, sir."

He then asked, "Did you hit him more than once…say…while he was on the floor?"

I responded truthfully, "No, sir, one punch was all."

Then he said to me, "Well, it's a good thing you only hit him once because if you had continued to strike him after he hit his head, you'd be going to jail tonight. Wait here…"

I sensed that this wasn't over yet on account of the "wait here" command. That was when I was most apprehensive. What was my fate going to be that night? The next thirty minutes dragged on slowly.

Gigantor went out and radioed the emergency room to check on the guy's status. On returning, he was holding one of those heavy aluminum folding clipboards—the kind that hold forms. He told me, "That guy is in bad shape. He has lacerations to the head that will require stitches and a shattered orbit that's going to require surgery. He's going to be hurting for a while. He's also going to be charged with assault…if you want to press charges…?"

I sensed that the officer was hoping that my answer would be no, which it was. Was I really going to waste my time driving down to Roosevelt for a trial? No way.

Then the officer opened the clipboard and handed me a piece of paper and said, "Keep this in case that loser thinks he has grounds to sue you. You're free to go."

I had noticed the guy's buddies were eyeing me the whole time I was talking to the officer, so I asked him, "Uh, would you mind doing me a favor? Would you keep those guys here until you can't hear my bike anymore?"

He knew *exactly* what I was asking and said, "I'm sure it'll take me at least an hour to interview them. You're good…"

I noticed the slightest hint of a grin from that tough-as-nails Utahn giant as I excused myself and headed out the door. After stuffing the paperwork into the Tour Pak, I jumped on my bike and made it to my motel.

With the adrenaline pumping during and after the actual event, I never felt anything after knocking that guy to the floor. But man, my hand hurt in the morning—it was purple and throbbing! I then had a decision to make—continue on to the North Rim of Grand Canyon, another four hundred-plus miles, or start to double back north to Cody, four hundred-plus miles in the other direction. I decided to continue south. But first, I read the paperwork the officer had given me; my curiosity needed satisfaction.

In a nutshell, the paper stated that I had used appropriate force in defending myself from an "imminent battery." Hot damn! Now I wouldn't have to worry for months after whether I might get an unwelcome phone call from some lawyer or maybe get a subpoena for a civil action against me for that guy's medical bills. That news was a good way to start the day's riding.

A rider's right hand is his throttle and brake hand. It gets exercised continually while riding and even more so in traffic while alternately rolling on and off the throttle and working the brake. By the time I made it to the North Rim, where I had a room reserved, my entire wrist and halfway up my arm were black and blue—not good. *Could I have broken my hand?* I wondered.

Braking had become painful. I could no longer squeeze the brake lever normally but instead had to hover my wrist over the grip and press my fingertips toward my thumb. Planning my stops was no problem, and this awkward braking worked well enough to ride safely—as long as I didn't have to crush the brakes suddenly like when a car runs in front of you without warning.

The next morning, my wrist was barely discolored, and I felt little discomfort due likely to the four shots-and-beers and four Tylenol I had slammed before bed. I did feel a bit of pain while loading up the bike and tightening the straps that secured my load, but other than that, it was an awesome day without a cloud in the sky. I started back north to Bryce Canyon National Park where I would spend the night. Bryce is fairly close to Grand, so I spent the day doing side trips. As the day went on, my wrist and the back of my hand became deep purple again—a sure sign of internal bleeding/bruising. By then, braking had become difficult.

The next day, I slept late to nurse my aching hand. I decided to ride straight on back to Cody—seven hundred-plus miles. Regrettably, I got the added treat of monsoon rains for much of the ride, although the cold rain actually felt good on my swollen hand.

I was doing okay until about seventy-five miles from my cottage. It was past three o'clock in the morning, and the storms had kept most of the deer down, which was one less thing to worry about while riding solo at night in remote country. But that was also wildfire season.

Wildfires tend to drive game out of its natural habitat, and you never know what you'll see in the oddest places. And so it was that night.

I was thinking after gassing up in Thermopolis, *It's a straight shot from here—almost home.*

Moments later, two coyotes were bounding straight at me, chasing a rabbit that no doubt was burned out of its brushy home. I instinctively crushed the brakes to avoid a collision, only without the deliberate alternate hand positioning that I had been using for the last thousand miles or so.

The pain shot up my arm and actually felt like a blow to my neck. I almost dumped the bike before I got safely to the shoulder. I no longer had any grip strength to hold the bike up if it started to fall to the right. I became nauseated because the pain was so great, and I developed instantly an intense throbbing headache.

I dismounted my bike and put my head down between my knees for what seemed like forever. After a good while, that eased the nausea enough that I saddled up, restarted the bike, and then pulled away slowly. That last seventy-five miles took forever because instead of running at sixty-five—the legal limit at that time—I kept it under fifty just in case something else jumped out on the road ahead of me.

When I arrived at my cottage around 5:00 a.m., I didn't even unpack the bike. I went in, took a handful of Tylenol, and went to bed. On waking, much of the swelling had gone down, but unlike the two prior mornings where the purplish color had subsided overnight, my hand and wrist were as black as could be. I headed off to the clinic—on foot—to have them confirm what I was already sure was the diagnosis: one or more broken bones.

X-ray techs are not permitted to interpret the radiographs— only a physician is supposed to tell you what's up. On asking whether I had any broken bones, the young tech just smiled and said the doctor would be in shortly before saying, "I can't believe you rode a motorcycle with *that*!" as I glimpsed at the screen over her shoulder.

That was confirmation enough. She knew that I knew—before the physician told me—I had suffered a "boxer break." You know—the kind you get when punching a wall when drunk…or punching a drunk into a floor…in a club…in Utah.

The damage required surgery with pins protruding through my hand under a cast for six weeks, and consequently, I was done riding until mid-September when the cast was removed. Despite the physician assistant telling me to take it easy for a while before starting physical therapy, I literally got home from the clinic the day the cast was removed, loaded the bike, and headed to Reno, Nevada, for the Street Vibrations Rally.

I figured *using* my hand as I would do normally was the best physical therapy, right!

JUST ENOUGH GAS

Back in 2007, I went to the Street Vibrations Rally in Reno, Nevada. I left the same day I had a cast removed from my right hand, which was earned because of a bar fight down in Utah six weeks earlier that had resulted in a boxer break.

Because the broken hand denied me most of Wyoming's good riding season, I was hell-bent to make that trip. I packed the bike in no time. I made sure I had plenty of layers, my rain gear, and my lined leather riding gloves, just in case it got cold before I returned to Cody. The last thing I packed was a 1.1 gallon plastic gas can, which I secured to one of the passenger running boards, because there are some mighty long stretches in Utah and Nevada between gas stops, especially on US 50.

Mid-September weather in my neck of the woods can be a crapshoot. It might be in the midseventies and sunny, or you could be shoveling inches of snow. When I left for Reno, it was the former—warm and sunny all the way the first day.

While I prefer to head down to US 50—America's Loneliest Road—I rode mostly I-80 instead, for the sake of making time, so I could add in certain side trips besides Reno itself.

One must-see stop for me was Virginia City, Nevada. This historic silver mining town had been almost singly responsible for financing the Civil War. Plus, I am a Mark Twain fan and wanted to see his office where he had once worked for the local newspaper. There's lots of history there, lots to see and do.

The temperature had dropped dramatically overnight the first day of the trip, and on the ride up to Virginia City, there was fresh snow along the shoulders of the road. But the road itself was only wet. The temperature was in the low forties on the way up the hill.

I wasn't in any particular hurry, so I putted along at a leisurely pace. After a while, I was passed by about a dozen Hells Angels, who were flogging it through a long straightaway to get all their riders past me.

After a while, I rode up on the tail Angel in their group once we were in the twisties. I thought, *What the hell!* These *guys can't handle curvy roads?*

My good friend Gabby won't hang back for slow riders—whether three-patch one-percenters or otherwise—so I guess I got my more aggressive riding style from riding with him. I started to look through the turns for a shot to pass.

I held back passing however on seeing a pair of little bikes—maybe 350s at best—whose riders were embarrassingly intimidated by the curves…or the wet roads…or the remaining snow…or all three, probably.

My restraint was only short-lived. I was fed up going thirty to thirty-five miles an hour, and I was amazed that the dozen or so Angels put up with that shit too. However, a good road captain won't pass unless there's room enough to get his whole group around, together. I figured that was the only reason the Red and White held back. But not me.

I flogged the throttle once I could see through a couple of turns. I scraped the right running board while I leaned so far over and back into the lane the two pokey riders were occupying, on the outside of a turn. They freaked out and hit the brakes hard with Angels piling up on their backsides. That was the last thing I saw in my mirrors as I tore ass through the remaining curves into Virginia City.

Parking during any rally can be hit or miss. As I rolled through the main drag in town, I scouted for a spot to park the Electra Glide. The first available spot I found big enough for my bagger was way down the street in front of the Bucket of Blood Saloon.

Virginia City's altitude contributed to the noticeably lower temperature from that along the road up the hill. I was cold and decided to add a layer under my leather jacket rather than head right into the saloon. While I was fumbling around in my saddlebag, I heard the rumble of the pack of Angels that was just then getting to town. I glanced down the street and saw that they decided to park right on the last bend at the edge of town where they could fit all their bikes together.

I noticed too that one of the Angels—their lead rider—was bounding up the street straight toward me. Hmm…was this guy pissed off because I closely passed his group on the turns? Was he coming to "educate" me? You just never know with one-percenters.

I reached deeper into my saddlebag for the 1911A1 .45 Colt pistol I carried back then. I kept it concealed but cocked the hammer—just in case.

To my utter shock, the first words out of that behemoth's mouth were "Hey, man, thanks for passing those two assholes back there! They had no clue anyone else was behind them until you did. After you blew by them, they woke up and pulled over to let us by."

I replied, "Shit, man, I *had* to. My bike leans more on the kickstand in the garage than those two could lean into a turn!"

Mr. Angel roared laughing, and then extended his hand. I de-cocked the big Colt and quickly withdrew my hand from my saddlebag and shook his hand.

Holy shit! My hand had only just seen the light of day after six weeks pinned in a cast. That guy believed in a firm handshake as I do. Man, my hand was screaming. Still, it was a sincere gesture from a giant one-percenter—no harm intended. That set the tone for a great day to follow.

I ate lunch in the Bucket of Blood before heading out on the mostly covered boardwalk streets in this National Historic Landmark city. There were all manner of vendors, selling anything from tourist-trap crap to high-end antiques and Native American jewelry. It was there I saw "White Buffalo" turquoise for the first time—interesting stuff.

I did a bit of the "tourist thing"—that is, I took a couple of the for-pay tours to comprehend the significance of this midnineteenth century city that existed decades before Wyoming was even a state. And I saw the very desk at which Mark Twain had sat during his stint in this once-tumultuous Western metropolis. He described his dangerous cross-country trek via stagecoach to reach Virginia City in *Roughing It*, one of his all-time classic works.

I spent the night at a quaint bed-and-breakfast at the far end of town. I noticed a lot of old vacant houses that looked like they would be great to own—until I inquired about them to the B&B owners. They told me there is significant danger of cave-ins or landslides at that end of town. Apparently, mining took place right under the town. Much of the above-ground city is supported only by the stepped and stoped tunnels beneath the streets, which some civil engineers would condemn because the support timbers have shifted and decayed.

Yikes! I had visions of the final scenes of *Paint Yer Wagon* as No-Name City collapses into the hidden underground tunnel complex dug by Lee Marvin and Clint Eastwood. I wondered whether one minor earthquake would be the end of town.

Well, I didn't dwell on the possibility of the End of Days but instead enjoyed the company of my hosts, their fine food, and the company of some other bikers from Cali who were staying there as well.

Before heading to Reno the next day, I made a side trip over to Donner Pass, where the party of the same name resorted to cannibalism rather than starve to death during the bitter cold snow bound winter of 1847. I thought, *Hardly a "party"!*

The following day, I sidetracked further still, despite forecasts for a cold front coming through. I headed up to Lake Tahoe and rode the loop around the lake on both the Nevada and California sides. I had hoped to see where *The Godfather* was filmed but never found the property. I had some awesome meals in the Tahoe area before heading east, albeit earlier than I had planned thanks to the abruptly changing weather.

The temperature had already dropped from the high sixties into the forties with heavy cloud cover rolling in. It was a sure thing I wouldn't make it back to Cody without wearing rain gear somewhere along the way. Rather than extend my road trip into the approaching front, I pointed my bike east.

It was a cold and gloomy ride all the way to Battle Mountain, Nevada, where I stopped for the night. The major sources of income in Battle Mountain are gold mining and donating your "gold" to the small-scale casinos. If I were a betting man, I'd bet another undocumented source of income is meth trafficking, based on all the rotten-tooth meth-head tweakers I ran into.

I found a cheap motel on the main drag. I off-loaded my bike and walked across the street to one of their tiny casinos that had a diner-like restaurant attached. I don't remember what I ordered, and I didn't recognize what I got either. It appeared to have been made of meat, slathered with enough burned gravy to warrant shutdown by the American Heart Association. I choked it down and washed the taste of it from my mouth with two twelve-ounce Pepsis before walking to the C-store to get some junk food to supplement that god-awful casino fare.

By the time I made it back to my room, it had started raining gently. The storm front that I had managed to stay ahead of all day had caught up to me.

I was awoken before daybreak by the wind-driven rain beating on the window by my bed. It was useless to try to get back to sleep.

So I got up, showered, and dressed, including a set of Merino wool long johns because the TV weather reported just thirty-eight degrees outside. Over my jeans, I added my leather chaps. Up top I put on a heavy denim shirt, a zip-neck fleece vest, and finally my reliable Windstopper lined wool sweater before adding my leather jacket. Over everything, I put on my rain gear. It was going to be a cold, wet, shitty ride to Rock Springs, where I had hoped to make it for the night.

On the road, I usually carry two helmets: a "compliance" shell, which is just enough to keep the local police from stopping you in helmet states like Nevada, and a useful three-quarter helmet with a flip-up face shield for protection in cold or wet weather. I put on the three-quarter, and then my lined black leather Carhartt gloves, and out the door I went.

Battle Mountain sits at about 4,500 feet. While it was raining on me, the upper half of the outlying mountains had become snow-covered overnight. I had higher country to cross between there and Cody, so I was hoping the temps would rise as the day went on.

Interstate riding in the rain isn't all that bad so long as you keep dry. Keeping dry was easy with the combination of helmet and Harley Gore-Tex rainsuit, although the Carhartt leather gloves were soaked through and provided little warmth for my hands. The late September traffic was light—mostly the occasional tractor-trailer. I made it to Rock Springs late in the day and managed to keep warm down to thirty-five degrees, the lowest temp indicated on the analog gauge that I had added to the '05 Electra Glide.

While you can certainly ride safely all day in the rain, it just sucks! It gets downright depressing when going cross country and you ride all day in the rain, get off your bike for the night in the rain, and then you get up to more rain and do it all over again the next day. That is what I did returning to Cody back in 2007. Well, not exactly—that would have been preferred to the all-day on-again-off-again rain/snow I rode through on that last day!

Rather than head toward Lander—the shortest route back from Rock Springs—I headed farther east to avoid the high country over South Pass that was getting hammered with snow. I figured that by heading up through Muddy Gap and over to Sweetwater Station, I wouldn't go through the highest country and could avoid most of the heavy snow.

My plan was to exit the interstate at Rawlins, and then head northwest. I was eager to get off the Super Slab because the Wyoming two-lanes would have virtually no traffic and so one less hazard to contend with.

The interstate portion was challenging to say the least. I always wondered how accurate the temperature gauge was that I had added to my bike. Well, I found out on that trip. Every time the gauge dropped to thirty-two, the rain would slush up into wet snow. At thirty, it was all snow!

Besides the obvious concern over riding a one-wheel-drive two-wheeler on slushy roadway at highway speeds, sharing the roads with eighteen-wheelers and inattentive cagers, I then also had to contend with visibility issues. Every time I exhaled, the face shield would fog over. Plus, with the sideways wind, I was looking through four layers of beading water droplets—one on each side of my face shield and another pair on my glasses.

I must admit, the cagers and truckers gave me a wide berth, but probably only because they were worried I could slide under their wheels at any moment. That was a possibility although slight. I was really impressed at how well the Dunlop tires cut through the slush and tracked safely.

When I rolled into Rawlins, I was going to get gas. But the wind and wet snow were blowing sideways, and I didn't want water getting in the tank as I pumped fuel. I decided I had enough gas to fuel up in Jeffrey City, and maybe by then, the wind would subside.

Just as I made the turn at Muddy Gap toward Jeffrey City, the bike stuttered and coughed—I switched to reserve quickly and kept rolling.

In about twenty-five miles, I rolled into Jeffrey City and...*screw me*! The singular gas station that I knew about—and where I had fueled up just the preceding summer—was closed, along with everything else in that uranium mining ghost town! I had no choice but to press on with what little fuel I had left on reserve.

About halfway between Jeffrey City and the junction at Sweetwater Station, I pulled into an overlook. Wind and rain be damned—I needed fuel. I poured the contents of my auxiliary gas bottle into the tank after I headed the fairing into the wind. Between that and the fuel door, I kept most of the water from getting into the tank. I could only hope the added fuel would be enough to get me to Lander or Riverton, whichever was closer.

I was fighting fierce headwinds along most of that route, so I throttled back to fifty miles an hour to conserve fuel. Just before the junction, I saw a sign: Lander 24, Riverton 22. I turned on Sand Draw road toward Riverton.

Just after making that turn, the road rose abruptly for a mile or so. As I rose, the ground became completely snow-covered, although the road remained mostly wet with just a little slush. When I crested the hill, it was like hitting a wall of warm air—well, if you consider forty degrees warm, that is. The wind was gone on the downside too. However, the warm air over the cold wet snow created white-out fog.

Shit! I had used too much fuel to double back toward Lander. I could only press on.

I put my flashers on, shifted into neutral, shut off the engine, and coasted for more than a mile at times—on every downslope toward Sand Draw. By then, only rain fell for the rest of the ride to Cody. The only thing I had to worry about then was getting run over from behind by someone traveling much faster through the fog than the forty to fifty miles an hour I could maintain while coasting.

Eventually, I recognized the familiar junction with Gas Hills road, which meant I was only a mile or two from the first gas station in Riverton. Just as I approached the gas pump, my engine died—it was out of gas completely!

I pumped 5.2 gallons into the nominal five-gallon tank, which was half a gallon more than I'd ever pumped before while my gauge was bottomed out.

I had just enough fuel with the gas bottle and from coasting and riding slowly to make it to Riverton for precious gas and a place to get warm. I never want to repeat that run. I can tell you that!

I rolled into my cottage on the Richards' ranch back in Cody, peeled off my clothes, and slept straight through the night. I was cold and exhausted but smiled as I dozed off, knowing that I had beaten the road—one more time.

The maddening thing about my whole snowy ride is that it could have been avoided. In Reno, I had run into my friend Thad. Thad invited me to stay with him at his dad's place for the week. By the time Thad rode home, the cold front had passed, and he rode home in eighty-degree weather almost the whole way!

Smell Like a Rose

"Boy, you could step in shit and still come out smelling like a rose!"

My father used to say that to me after I had just emerged unscathed from some misadventure that usually cost him and my mother a few gray hairs. I got away with a lot of risky behavior most of my life—calculated risks, pushing up to limits. Truth be told, I could have been killed or maimed lots of times just doing the things I find are just plain living—especially riding "murdercycles" as the old man called them. It's ironic that I never broke any bones until I was thirty-three. And that was when I slipped going down an icy bank while winter fishing—not exactly a risky undertaking, ordinarily!

Since 2015, I have been in two motorcycle crashes that have resulted in over twenty broken bones, including massive facial trauma and skull damage, despite wearing helmets. Not exactly smelling like a rose, Dad!

Despite the long road to recovery from both incidents, there have been a number of silver linings too. When I was ten years old, I was pushed off my friend's front porch while horsing around. When I landed, my head was snapped to my chest; I nearly blacked out. Later that summer, while visiting my cousins—with whom I always got into mischief—we were using the swings at the local park to swing as high as possible, nearly vertical, before bailing out to see how far we could sail through the air. Well, my best distance ever came at a price. When I landed, I again snapped my chin to my chest; I was in agony.

My cousins were mortified, not over me, but over the parental wrath that would surely befall us all when we got back to their house—but only if the folks found out.

So we stayed at the park for an hour more, long enough for me to stand and breathe normally, although I had intense tingling in both arms. We came in quietly through the back door and avoided the folks. It worked—no one ever knew about my aerial acrobatics and the unplanned outcome. That was probably a mistake because from that time forward, I would have severe episodes of back pain so intense at times I would fall to the floor because simple breathing felt like a knife being plunged and twisted in my back. I had learned to live with that until July of 2015 because no doctor could ever pinpoint the cause.

When "Bulwinkle" decided to occupy a piece of roadway in front of my motorcycle traveling at sixty-five miles an hour, it didn't end well. I broke eight ribs in my back, some vertebrae, both wrists, my occipital bone, my right orbit, and I lost a couple of teeth—fifteen bones altogether. Plus, my cherished 1998 FLHTCI, with 209,000 miles on the clock, was totaled. What possible silver lining could come from that?

Since then, my back has only gone out once. It was a pinched nerve, unrelated to my head snap at age ten. So it would seem that forty-four years of back pain were terminated by rolling down an embankment like a rag doll. I can't recall how many weekends or vacations were ruined while I was in back pain over the years, and so leaving that all behind is a pretty good silver lining if you ask me. A pretty "rosy" ending to a murdercycle ride, eh, Dad?

Then again, when I got clipped by an uninsured SUV driver at eighty miles an hour in Salt Lake City in September of 2019 and "donated" another bike to the insurance company as a result—my 2014 FLHTCU—and then spent a month in the hospital getting just well enough to leave in a wheelchair, what silver lining could possibly result from that?

I'll tell you: I'm alive—that's what—and mobile again too!

I beat incredible odds. I went down at eighty miles an hour without a steel backboard riding suit with padded body armor. My face was caved in, after which I slid for 150 feet. I lost a metacarpal bone in my left hand that's been replaced with cadaver bone. My jaws were wired shut for two months. I only ate through a straw. The arch bars (surgical braces) saved all but three of my teeth. My ankles were broken. My left leg was crushed, and the pieces are held in place with screws that hold a titanium pipe running full-length inside my tibia.

Since the crash, my face has been reconstructed with four titanium plates and more screws than I can count in the X-rays.

Still, *someone* must have been looking out for me because I usually don't wear a helmet. Only just minutes before that crash, however, I had stopped to put on a new half-shell that I bought only because it had an internal flip-down sunscreen, which I needed that day because I was heading into the late afternoon western sun. That helmet was destroyed; the gashes in it would have been in my skull instead. However, that half-shell couldn't protect my face from being caved in on striking the concrete.

The lead trauma team doctor later told me that it was a good thing I *hadn't* been wearing a full-face helmet even though it would have protected my face. He explained that if I had been wearing a full-face lid, because of the way my face hit the pavement, its chin bar would have snapped my neck, leaving me dead or a quadriplegic! To me, being a quad and becoming a burden to my wife for the rest of my life would be worse than dying—I'll take a reconstructed face any day. And that's my silver lining for this crash. It's not the rosiest of endings, but today, I am walking and riding again!

And...there's always more fun to be had...

LAUGHTER IN DISASTER

In the week leading up to the seventy-fifth annual Sturgis Rally in 2015, I had a good friend from my Rogue Hog days ride out from Delaware to visit me in Cody. Let's just call him "Paul J." The name has been changed slightly to protect...the guilty! Paul is sixty-seven years old and is the biggest pothead I've ever met. But hey, "live and let live," I always say. And just as with my maximum-laughs-per-mile friend Gabby, Paul can be...let's just say..."entertaining" on the road!

We had planned to ride our Harleys through Yellowstone and the Tetons while he was out to visit, but the cam chain and cam bearings were shot in the bottom end of his motor. So instead of chancing a blown engine miles from the nearest dealer or tow vehicle or aborting our trip, I told Paul to ride my '98 FLH while I would take my '14 FLH. It wasn't the first time I would loan Paul the '98 Electra Glide. He had ridden it back in '99 one night while his trusty '77 FLH Shovelhead was down for one reason or another. In fact, that ride was what convinced Paul to buy a new Twin Cam FLHTCU in 2000—the very bike he was on that summer.

So in addition to warmer layers, rain gear, and a boatload of chocolate Tootsie pops, Paul loaded up my '98 with a few vials of his best weed. "Vial" is a bit misleading here. Paul's vials were more like miniature Mason jars!

The absolute best times I have had group riding were with the Rogue Hogs. We logged countless tens of thousands of miles on weekend putts and the occasional weekend getaways. During most of that time, I remember Paul and others taking time out to blaze a joint or bowl during our longer rest stops. Paul was the center of attention and not just because he was generous with his stash but because he always had the most amazing true-life stories to spin, which often left us wondering how he survived past thirty. Even those Rogues who didn't smoke or drink always had a good time on the road with Paul.

It would be no different for that trip where it was just me and Paul. Paul hadn't been out my way before, so I was the de facto road captain. I had planned for him to see some of the most noteworthy scenery to be viewed from the saddle of a Harley while he was visiting. So on Wednesday, July 29, we headed out from my house in Cody.

Over the next day and a half, I led Paul over the Beartooth Highway, the highest road in Wyoming and the highest paved road in the Northern Rockies, through Wind River Canyon, Yellowstone, and Grand Teton National Parks and on a lot of local riding in between.

Periodically, Paul would relax with a bowl of his best. That never bothered me and even while he was riding one of my bikes. The saying, "There are old bikers, and there are stoned bikers. But there are no old stoned bikers"—meaning that you die before you get old if you ride high—just didn't seem to apply to Paul. He might possibly be one of those rare exceptions where being relaxed from smoking makes him a *better* rider.

On the second day, we finished dinner in Jackson Hole and decided to ride all the way back to Cody rather than get a ridiculously overpriced motel room.

We got back to my house after midnight. When we did, I wanted to be certain that Paul got his vials out of the Tour Pak on the '98. No way did I want to get busted for possession during a traffic stop for *his* leftover weed, especially considering I didn't even smoke.

"Paul, be sure you get your stash out of my bike."

"Oh yeah, I think there are two or three vials left."

"Is it *two* or *three*, Paul! I don't need any surprises!"

He just laughed and reached in the open Tour Pak and, in the dim driveway light, grabbed the vials that remained from the start of our trip.

The next day, Paul headed east to Sturgis to meet other friends of ours, and Stacey and I would head to Sturgis too to join up with them, although separately from Paul, later that day.

Even though I had the newer '14 FLH, Stacey preferred the seating on the old '98, which had been Paul's loaner. So I packed up the bike, and we headed out late in the day after Stacey finished work.

Stacey and I never made it to Sturgis for the seventy-fifth. About 8:00 p.m. on July 31, a cow moose decided to cross our path and stop in her tracks in our lane. The moose was just thirty yards from us when it walked out from the swale on the side of the road. I couldn't swerve to the left; there was an oncoming truck. All I could do was bleed off as much speed as possible before laying the bike down. We had to avoid hitting the moose because they stand five to six and a half feet high at the shoulder and we would have died from the sudden stop—it's that simple.

I don't remember hitting the ground, but the witnesses in the car that was behind us said that my helmet strap broke off on the first hit, which explains why I sustained a shattered right orbit and fractured basal skull bone. Anyway, the first responders were the people in the car behind us. As luck would have it, they had more first aid equipment in their vehicle than the EMTs who arrived before the ambulance, and they knew how to use it.

I was in absolute agony with pain radiating from my back. I would later learn that I had fractured two vertebra and eight ribs. The pain in my back was so great that night that I felt nothing from my shattered left wrist, which allowed my hand to flop over like it was on a hinge. I remember telling one of the responders—none of whom I could see from the blood that was running in my eyes from the head injuries—that I thought my wrist was broken as he tried frantically to remove my watch, whose bracelet was cutting into the swollen flesh.

I also remember calling out for Stacey. Thankfully, someone was attending to her too. She hadn't broken any bones but suffered severe road rash. I was grateful she wasn't injured as badly as I, and on learning that, I relaxed quite a bit.

Despite learning that Stacey was in fair shape, I suddenly panicked. Would I walk again? I raised my head enough to see my feet through blood-blurred vision, and I waved them in and out. I remember relaxing then and thinking, *This will pass.*

By then, there was a WHP trooper on scene. Shortly after, the strangest thing happened. Right within earshot of the Trooper, the first responder bent down over me and, in a low voice, said, "Hey, buddy, is there any paraphernalia in your bike you want me to get rid of for you?"

I responded immediately, "No."

And why wouldn't I? I had nothing to hide.

And then it hit me. *Oh, shit! What if Paul had missed one of his "Mason jars" the night before while emptying the Tour Pak of his stuff?*

There'd be *no way* I would ever convince the WHP trooper—or a jury—that the stuff wasn't mine and that it belonged to a visiting friend. It'd be like trying to convince your fourth-grade teacher that your past-due term paper had been eaten by your dog!

I started to laugh uncontrollably. Now, let me tell you. Breathing with broken ribs is agony. Laughing should have made me black out—it was that much worse.

And all the while, I was cussing my friend Paul, who had no idea I was lying in a ditch wondering whether there *might be* some paraphernalia left behind in my now-totaled FLH.*

They say laughter is the best medicine—just not with broken ribs. The uncertainty over whether I might have had Paul's leftovers in my bike was absolutely hilarious to me in the moment. So even though Paul was hundreds of miles away, he was responsible for me having a few more laughs on the road. Yeah, literally *on* the road!

---

* What makes this even funnier now is that I learned later that the first responder who offered to "destroy evidence" for me was a retired Illinois sheriff!

WHAT'RE FRIENDS FOR?
(PART 1)

While thinking of the many adventures I've created in the saddle of my now-totaled '98 and '14 Electra Glides, I smile at how many of them involved my good friend Gabby and the funny shit that always seemed to happen when we went on the road together. To sum up Gabby in a word: *intense*!

Gabby is quite possibly the only other rider I've known who is more passionate about riding than I am. Then again, Gabby is intense with everything he does. When Gabby gets it in his mind to do a certain thing, there is no stopping him—whether for a one-time event or sticking to certain of his routines. More often than not, Gabby was the only other one of the Rogue Hogs besides me who could be found riding all winter long until ice and snow would park us for a week or two at a time.

Gabby had always liked tinkering on his bikes. In the old days, in a given week, he might have been pushing the limits of performance by jetting his carburetor on the fat side. In the very next week, he'd be pursuing the highest possible mileage by re-jetting the carb on the lean side. On one of his high-mileage kicks, he blew the engine in his trusty '87 Tour Glide.

In an internal combustion engine, a leaner burn is a hotter burn. Gabby had jetted the carb so lean on the Tour Glide that at eighty to ninety miles an hour on the interstate, he suddenly lost power and the bike was blowing smoke from the pipes like a mosquito sprayer. The bike ran so hot that it melted a hole the size of a quarter in one of the pistons!

Such a catastrophic engine failure would dishearten most riders, but not Gabby. While he could break most anything on a bike, he could as easily fix anything too once back in his garage. I suppose his wrenching and fabrication skills are what I admire most about him. He's a great friend and responsible for more laughs per mile than anyone else I know.

So between his intensity for riding and his ability to wrench—whether on the road or back in the garage—it only seemed logical for me to invite him to join me on my first registered Iron Butt run, which he gladly accepted.

The Iron Butt Association is dedicated to the sport of safe, long-distance motorcycle endurance riding. The minimum criteria for becoming a member is completing the Saddle Sore 1000—riding one thousand miles or more in twenty-four hours or less. This must be documented with time- and location-stamped toll, meal, or gas receipts and signed odometer witness forms at the start and end of the run. For a little more of a challenge, one can do the Bun Burner 1500, 1,500 miles or more in thirty-six hours or less, or the Bun Burner Gold, 1,500 miles or more in twenty-four hours or less. Finally, each year there is the Iron Butt Rally, which, in the first year I was an IBA member, consisted of a minimum of 11,000 miles in eleven days. The IBA was just our sort of organization, although most of our long runs went undocumented because neither Gabby nor I care about proving ourselves to anyone. We know our exploits in the saddle, and for us, that is enough. In fact, I don't think Gabby ever turned in his paperwork for the Saddle Sore 1000 we completed together. He just doesn't care because he knows he is one of the long riders of our generation.

Now, because I knew too well Gabby's tendency to tinker on his bike up to the last minute before a run, I asked him to be sure he'd gotten all of his tinkering out of his system and to validate his bike the week ahead of the trip and to have his bike loaded and ready to roll at 3:00 a.m. the Friday morning we would leave for Sturgis 2000. He agreed. That was a relief because even though he could fix most anything along the side of the road that he might have caused by his incessant tinkering, we couldn't afford lost time for a pit stop during a registered run on a very deliberate route.

Every year while I lived in Delaware and rode to Sturgis, I would leave between 2:00 a.m. and 3:00 a.m. This was because I was too pumped up to get any sleep and because leaving at that hour would avoid traffic around certain eastern cities and would have me in higher country in the mountains of Western Pennsylvania before the heat of an August day. This plan worked well for me the many awful years I lived in Delaware and was what Gabby and I had agreed to do together.

Around 2:00 a.m., I got out of bed, along with my very supportive wife Stacey, who signed the Iron Butt affidavit, attesting to the mileage on my already-loaded bike and the start time. I rolled the '98 Electra Glide out of the garage, and the last thing I saw was Stacey smiling at me as she closed the garage door as I rolled away. That set the tone for what would surely be a great first day on my way to Sturgis 2000 and a two-week-plus run with Gabby…until I rolled up to his house, that is.

As I approached Gabby's house, I could see the light illuminating his driveway from the open garage door.

Great, I thought, *he's ready to roll.*

But as I rolled up the driveway, my blood began to boil. I was in utter disbelief at the scene before me. Gabby's bike was in the lift, missing one saddlebag, and not even loaded yet!

I yelled into the house at the top of my lungs, "WHAT THE HELL!"

One of Gabby's characteristic traits is his adherence to certain routines. He will have his morning coffee or herbal tea no matter what. To ensure this during our trip, he had purchased one of those resistance-element one-cup water heaters—the kind you drop into a cup of water to heat it up directly. He had the saddlebag off the bike to connect it to the battery directly to test how well it would heat water and without the bike running. This is why he wasn't packed by 3:00 a.m., despite his assurance he wouldn't tinker with the bike the week before the trip and be packed and ready to roll on my arrival.

This wouldn't have bothered me ordinarily, but I was already one hour into my allotted twenty-four for the Iron Butt by the time I rolled up in his driveway. He knew I was pissed off, and he packed quickly. We rolled out in under an hour, but before we did, I read him the riot act for making us late per our itinerary (and later felt guilty about it). But as he mounted his bike, I heard him mutter, "Hey, what're friends for!"

Not funny, Gabby!

Making time on an Iron Butt run can require exceeding the speed limit, but more than that, it requires smart riding and time management. For example, run the tank nearly out between fill-ups and make each gas stop also a bathroom, snack, and drink break. Also, *do not* speed excessively because you will lose time in more frequent gas stops. An Evo-engine Harley on weekend back-road putts at fifty to fifty-five miles an hour can get as much as fifty miles per gallon. However, that same bike at over eighty miles an hour can get only thirty-one to thirty-two miles per gallon. The increased frequency of gas stops can outweigh the faster time between them. For this reason, we kept to seventy miles an hour—a good balance between mileage and time. This allowed us in no-wind conditions to each get about 165 to 180 miles per tank before switching to reserve.

One of Gabby's pet peeves is riding in stop-and-go traffic. He'd rather jump off the highway the minute he rolls up on, for example, construction or an accident and reroute than spend ten minutes clutching the bike and banging gears. I don't blame him and usually followed him on some unfamiliar detour to beat traffic on many of our runs. But on this particular trip, it would be important to closely follow the deliberate route to our stopping place for the night because it was laid out to ensure we would at least meet the one thousand-mile Iron Butt minimum. Nevertheless, I can't exactly say I was surprised when, on coming into stop-and-go traffic on I-80 near the interchanges that run into Chicago, Gabby suddenly and without warning hauled ass down the shoulder and out of site! I was four lanes over and couldn't easily get to the shoulder if I wanted to.

I thought, *Great, Gabby, that's just great!*

I wasn't about to attempt to catch him. I followed the agreed-to route because I presumed he would eventually meet up with me later that day but certainly at the designated motel that night, which he knew of because I had given him a hand-written itinerary before we left.

Ironically, the traffic jam lasted less than fifteen minutes, and I was rolling free and easy again, albeit solo. Hopefully, Gabby got out of traffic his way and was en route as well all the way to Tomah, Wisconsin, for the night.

It was well after dark when I finally pulled off the Super Slab into a truck stop for a sit-down meal and to use a telephone (no cell phone back in 2000). I knew that any route that Gabby might have taken would run the risk of coming up short for his Iron Butt but also put him into the motel—which I had prepaid on my credit card—ahead of me. And *that*, I couldn't abide!

When you go on the road with others, you should stick together, despite a little stop-and-go traffic or any other unpleasant event along the way. And while I didn't mind riding solo—most of my long trips were alone—when you start out together, you stay together, or if in a group, individuals can peel off. But the group doesn't leave an individual. So it was then time for me to have a bit of fun at Gabby's expense.

I phoned the motel in Tomah and told the clerk I had met another rider on the road and I suspected that he would try to take my room from me on realizing that he had asked me many detailed questions about my ride to Sturgis, where I was staying for the night, and so on, which I foolishly answered. That was all bullshit, of course, but I went on to insist for that reason that *no one* be given a key to my room unless photo ID was presented *in my name only* and matched to my credit card. That would all but guarantee that Gabby would have no choice but to wait for me patiently—which he doesn't do well!

After my dinner, I rolled on toward Tomah. I had made good time and would surely hit my 1,100 mile goal well before the twenty-four-hour Iron Butt limit. So I slowed down to sixty miles an hour for two reasons: I had passed many road-killed deer carcasses and there were many grazing deer along the road's edge—no sense in speeding by these skittish animals on a bike. But the better reason for slowing down was how much longer I could protract Gabby's time without a place to go, waiting on me to catch up. Karma's a bitch!

I about pissed myself laughing when I finally rolled up to the motel entrance. Gabby was right in the registration lane, lying on his bike—head on the passenger seat, feet on the tank.

On seeing me, he yelled, "THESE PRICKS WOULDN'T LET ME IN THE ROOM!"

With a dead-pan look, I replied, "Huh, I wonder why?"

I never let on that I had blocked him out until over a year later, and when I did, I resisted telling him, "What're friends for!" Heh heh heh...that was funny, Gabby.

WHAT'RE FRIENDS FOR? (PART 2)

I've got to tell you. It was really hard not busting out laughing while Gabby continued to crank my ear about the motel staff not letting him in the room as we walked together up to the front desk. I laid my driver license up on the counter, gave the clerk my name, and showed my credit card, and only then did she give us keys to the room—exactly as I had requested over the phone from the truck stop. That was about 11:30 p.m. Central time, or twenty and a half hours after heading out. I had 1,106 miles on my bike, while Gabby had just over 1,000 because of his shortcutting from traffic on I-80 and because I live farther away than he does. I had Stacey's signed starting affidavit, and Gabby had gotten his signed by a clerk at a twenty-four-hour convenience store just outside of his neighborhood shortly after we rolled out. Now we just needed to find someone willing to verify our end mileage and sign our forms.

I asked the front desk clerk if she would mind signing our affidavits, after explaining what they were all about, and to step outside to verify our odometer readings on the form. She wanted nothing to do with it. Now maybe—just maybe—it had something to do with two do-rag-wearing bikers, filthy from a thousand hard miles on the road, who were asking a pretty young woman to "step outside and look at our bikes" late at night that triggered her internal danger alarm. She was visibly nervous while we hung around the lobby. In any case, we had made the run, and the clock was still ticking until we could get a witness to verify our mileage and time.

Then it occurred to me. The arrival time at the motel should be proof enough of our end time, and the IBA does route verification anyway based on the time- and location-stamped receipts along the way because certain foreign bikes' odometers can be off as much as 6 to 7 percent. So I returned to the front desk to ask for a printed check-in receipt. But it was then midnight, and no one was on the desk.

Dammit! All that whipping and driving for nothing, I thought.

As it turned out, midnight was shift-change time, and minutes later, another young woman took the desk. Oddly, on explaining our request to her, she never hesitated to verify and sign our forms. So with the Iron Butt run behind us, we could head off to get some sleep.

Despite running for almost a day straight, we both awoke the next morning ready to do it all over again. That was due in part to our natural stamina while on the road but more so from the machines we were riding.

Harley-Davidson touring bikes—whether an Electra Glide like mine (FLH) or a Tour Glide like Gabby's (FLT)—are built for comfort on the long haul and have been aptly nicknamed "road sofas." By comparison, there is no way I could have made an Iron Butt on my old FXE Shovelhead. Its rigid-mount motor would have vibrated my hands numb at highway speeds. The most I had ever ridden the Shovelhead in a day was around five hundred miles.

Probably the greatest source of fatigue on the rider is working the throttle and maintaining steady speed against the throttle return spring for hours at a time. On all non-cruise-control Harleys, however, this is made easier through the use of a throttle friction screw. By tightening down the screw to add some resistance to the throttle, you effectively have "pseudo cruise control." Sure, you still have to roll on and off the throttle as the terrain changes, but on the straightaways, little to no rider input is required. While the use of the friction screw can greatly reduce wrist fatigue, it must never be tightened to lock the throttle completely. Doing so could result in a fatal crash where the rider could not roll off the throttle in a hazardous situation. More on that later.

With 1,100 miles behind us on day 1, we then had two full days to make the remaining 700 miles or so to Sturgis—an easy riding pace. Day 2 should have been pretty uneventful as we rolled leisurely across the rest of Wisconsin and Minnesota, nearly to the South Dakota line. We could have made Sturgis on day two, but I had already booked a room in Luverne, Minnesota, for the second day.

Gabby and I packed the bikes early and had planned to grab breakfast before jumping back on the Super Slab. On cranking his FLT over, however, the starter barely turned—not enough speed to light the engine.

Shit! I thought. *Here we go...*

Gabby claimed to have bought a new battery just before the trip, but it was evident that the battery was weak and nearly dead. Because there was enough juice for the horn and console lights, we decided to "bump" start it. That required that I push his bike while fully loaded and with him in the saddle and the bike in second gear while he held the clutch in. Unfortunately for me, Gabby doesn't pack light! Bad enough pushing him and an eight hundred-pound bike, I had to move the added weight of his two weeks' worth of supplies for the road, including tools, which we never traveled without.

Eventually, however, I got him rolling with enough speed that we got the bike started on popping the clutch. Before I mounted my bike, I told him to be sure to park on a downslope thereafter until we could get his bike to a shop. He understood.

Despite not starting first thing in the morning, the bike started each time we stopped for gas along our route to Luverne. Something as simple as a loose connection on the starter could account for that behavior, but we couldn't be sure without tearing into the electrics. Neither of us wanted to do that along the roadside, and as long as the bike would run, Gabby was hesitant to find a shop to tap his wallet. So we pressed on.

For all the years I went to the Sturgis rally except for '81, I never actually stayed in Sturgis. Instead, I preferred to take to the high ground in the Black Hills and camp out where it is much cooler than in the hot and dusty makeshift rally-only campgrounds down in Sturgis and the surrounding prairie. For several years including 2000, I stayed at Kemp's Kamp, which is a nice family-oriented campground tucked up in a small side canyon off the main canyon along the Old Hill City road. I told Gabby that it would be ideal if we arrived well before sunset so that we would have enough light to pitch camp because it gets pretty dark in the canyon well before sundown. That had been our plan, anyway.

Gabby's bike failed to crank on the morning of day 3 as we were leaving Luverne. So like the day before, he bumped it. That time, however, he did it himself because he parked facing a downslope the night before.

The farther west we rode into South Dakota, the warmer it got. We were in the rolling prairie then with hot blasts of prairie wind, stripping the water from our hides at seventy-five miles an hour. Despite that, we decided to leave I-90 and jump on South Dakota 44. Route 44 goes through the Badlands where it would be even hotter and drier—although quite scenic—and it runs right up into the Hills on the way to Kemp's.

Gabby decided not to shut his bike off while getting fuel along that route because in that heat and without a downslope to bump the bike back to life, one or both of us would sweat our asses off trying to push-start his FLT. Leaving the bike running at idle for any length of time in the heat of summer is a risky thing to do to an air-cooled Harley engine because it can overheat quickly without air moving over the cylinders and heads.

Well within the interior of the Badlands, Gabby started to drop way back. So I would drop back until he would catch up. It wasn't unusual for him to roll off the throttle to take a moment to suck in the scenery while we were on the road, so I didn't think anything of it. But he was doing it so frequently it became very annoying. I finally decided to roll on at a steady pace. He could catch up any time he wanted—or so I thought.

Several minutes after Gabby had become a speck in my mirror, some guy came screaming up on his bike on the shoulder, yelling at me, "Hey, I think your buddy is broken down back there!"

I thought, *Shit, here we go again!*

I doubled back. In the short time Gabby was stopped, he had stripped his gear from the bike and had strewn the contents of his saddlebags along the shoulder, looking for his tool bag. He looked as pissed off as I was and perplexed because the bike just started to break up and finally quit running altogether—there was no spark. That confirmed that the battery was dead even though Gabby had just bought it the week before the trip.

So there we were, stuck in the treeless, shadeless prairie with the thermometer stuck on 105 degrees with a dead bike. There was only one solution: I had to ride all the way to the Harley dealer in Rapid City and buy a new battery for his bike, and then ride all the way back, get it installed, and hope that would get him moving again. And that's exactly what I did.

I probably pissed off every other rider on Route 44 on the way into and back from Rapid because I never went under a hundred miles an hour, weaving among the bikes as I came up on groups of riders along the way. But I had to be as quick as possible—my friend was stuck along the road in one hundred-plus-degree heat with little water and no shade. It was late afternoon, and we still needed to get to Kemp's before dark.

The Harley dealer during the rally is an absolute zoo with people everywhere. I got in the eight-row deep serpentine line to the parts counter, not even sure they might have the right battery for an '87. Nevertheless, after waiting in line for fifty minutes, I was able to score the right battery.

I asked, "Is it pre-charged with acid and charged up?"

"Yes," said the parts guy. So far so good.

I strapped the new battery to my already-overloaded bike and tore ass back into the Badlands. Well before I got to Gabby's bike, I saw three riders pull over, and then pull away without stopping—very strange.

On pulling up to Gabby, yet another rider was pulling over, apparently to aid this broken down rider, which most riders will do.

What hit me next was hilarious. There was Gabby, lying on his back in a ditch with his bike torn down on the right side and his belongings strewn about the shoulder like a bomb went off in his saddlebags. It looked like a bad wreck, and these people were stopping to help the apparent victim! When they rolled up, Gabby never got up—he just waved them off while lying on his back. It was funny as hell!

I noticed three vultures circling overhead. Apparently the motionless body below looked like a sure meal.

I yelled, "Gabby, look up!"

On opening his eyes, he sprang to his feet. "Shit! Those sons of bitches were eyeing me up! I better get moving!"

I about died laughing. Apparently, the prospect of becoming some raptor's next meal is a compelling motivator to get one's ass in gear!

There wasn't much two people could do, so I sat around while Gabby installed the new battery. Then he hit the starter and…nothing. He had console lights and a faint response from his horn. The supposedly charged battery was not!

The sun had set by then, and there were no more bikers coming from either direction. We were still stuck with a dead bike, and it was getting darker by the minute. In my hyper-focused run to get the battery and get back, I never thought to stop anywhere to buy more water. So there we were—hot, tired, and dehydrated while our minds went through the possible scenarios for getting his bike running again. At least by that time, the temperature had dropped…all the way to ninety-eight!

A sudden sinking feeling came over Gabby on realizing that he caused the problem the morning we left his house. I mistakenly thought he tried to run his water heater directly from the battery. He had not. That heater was a household 120-VAC unit. To use it with a 12-VDC motorcycle, he used a borrowed inverter, which, apparently when used while the engine was off, resulted in a fried rectifier! He had run his bike for two and a half days and around 1,600 miles on the battery alone, which is amazing, and all because he *just had to have* his morning coffee! At that point, all I could do was laugh.

After a short while, we saw lights approaching off in the distance. It was a car and a possible ride to town for Gabby and his gear. We were in luck. The driver was a young overeager summer ranger working in the Badlands. He stopped to render assistance. Luckily, he had jumper cables and cheerfully stayed long enough for us to get a decent charge into the new but weak battery.

After more than half an hour, the engine cranked to life. We packed Gabby's bike, thanked the ranger, and then sped to Rapid City, hoping to get to the dealer before they closed so they could test the charging system and so we could buy whatever parts it would take to fix the bike. Even though the dealer stays open quite late during the rally, we arrived just as they were closing their doors for the day.

We made it to Kemp's Kamp and set up in the dark, which had to be done cautiously because at each campsite there is a shingled shelter over the picnic table. The lower edge of these is only five feet and six inches to five feet and ten inches high, depending on the site—a real headbanger potential. We managed to avoid the hazard and turned in for a good night's rest on the ground.

The next day would be quite interesting for each of us.

WHAT'RE FRIENDS FOR? (PART 3)

Before Gabby and I set out for Sturgis 2000, which was almost nothing more than a brief stay-over in our overall two-and-a-half-week road trip, I told him in order to make it to all the scenic places I had lined out for our run, we would have to do a number of 500-plus mile days in the saddle. I reasoned that after getting the 1,100-mile Iron Butt leg of the trip behind us, that wouldn't be a problem. He agreed. I also told him that the real scenery begins in the Black Hills but only gets better the farther west we would go. Nevertheless, there are a number of must-do runs through the Hills any biker should complete during the rally. One in particular is Spearfish Canyon.

The Spearfish Canyon run begins outside of the town of Spearfish, South Dakota, and snakes its way through the Hills parallel to Spearfish Creek, a small cold-water trout stream, and winds over to Cheyenne Crossing, gaining altitude along the way. The route is actually old alternate US 14, and it runs into US 85, the Can Am highway. What makes that such an attractive run is the sheer cliff canyon walls and waterfalls and the lush green meadows and ponderosa pine trees in stark contrast to the surrounding prairie. Also, the route is one curve after another for 20 miles. In other words, our kind of road with plenty of pipe-dragger turns!

After limping into Kemp's in the dark, we were both exhausted from the heat of the Badlands the day before from coaxing Gabby's bike back to life. The resurrection was only temporary, however, without a working charging system. If Gabby were to go anywhere, he would have to get the bike fixed.

Ordinarily, I would be awake early while on the road, barring any late-night impromptu partying with new friends made along the way. But the morning after the Badlands adventure, neither Gabby nor I stirred until the whistle from the 1880 steam train across the creek from Kemp's sounded as it approached one of the twenty road crossings in the eleven-mile stretch between Keystone and Hill City. I jumped up, grabbed my fishing gear, and made off for Rapid Creek, one of the best trout streams in the Hills.

I felt bad for Gabby to have made it all that way only to be stranded at Kemp's. Because he was safely in camp with running water, had a place to crash, and it was a leisurely two-mile walk down the canyon to Keystone where there are dozens of restaurants and shops, I didn't feel like I was leaving a partner on the road. And besides, that was my vacation too, and I damn sure was going to get in some trout fishing.

After about a thirty-minute ride from camp, I spotted what appeared to be an ideal hole based on certain trout "prospecting" skills I had honed over years of fishing out-of-the-way streams in the mountains all over the United States. The spot I selected was well off the road in a section of Rapid Creek that transitioned from a skinny water swift-moving run straight into a solid stone cliff wall, where it made a ninety-degree bend before slowing and flattening again. At such places, the water scours out the bottom, forming deep pools with slower water, which form a natural feeding lane. Sure enough, after approaching slowly while keeping my shadow off the water, I could see through my polarized sunglasses twenty-five to thirty cruising trout, all about thirteen to fifteen inches in length and all rainbows. It was time to fish.

I almost exclusively practice catch-and-release fly fishing, but when "meat hunting," I'll use spinning tackle, whether with bait or lures. On the road, however, I only carry lures. I tied on a Panther Martin gold-blade black-bodied spinner, which, for reasons I cannot explain, will always coax more strikes from trout than any other color combination I have used.

As I got into position to cast to avoid the overhanging trees and brush, I noticed two behemoth trout lying at the bottom of the pool.

They were easily twenty inches each and football-fat in girth! Trout of that size in small water are truly exceptional. I cast toward those large hogs repeatedly but could not get my spinner down to their depth. Trout in food-rich streams will not move far for a meal—their food comes to them on the current. Nevertheless, while working these larger fish, I caught a half-dozen thirteen- to fifteen-inchers that were working higher in the water column. I released these, determined to land one of the footballs.

To get to the depth I needed, I began casting my spinner to the head of the pool, but instead of beginning the retrieve immediately, I let it sink to the bottom. I then immersed the tip of my rod into the water, just off the bottom of the streambed. On retrieving then, the spinner was hovering just off the bottom and in the strike zone of the fat ones. On the first cast, the larger of the two chased the lure for about three feet but did not strike.

Despite the first-cast tease, I couldn't get that fish to bite. However, that is not unusual—you can put a fish down after it detects a fake. Nevertheless, I cast over and over again to the same fish. Fifty casts soon became one hundred. A few times my lure even bumped the fish on the head. It would dart out of the way, and then take up its resting place all over again. That was maddening. My legs were getting numb from the crouched-down position I maintained to keep from spooking the fish with my shadow. Sooner or later, one of us was going to give out.

Famous salmon guide Eddie Martin once explained to me how he could catch so many king salmon in New York's Salmon River during the spawn despite the fact that kings do not eat during their spawning run. By using a lure called a hot shot—a deep-diving lure that shudders in the current—and holding it in the current from a drift boat right in a salmon's face, the salmon eventually strike. The theory is that they strike defensively—a sort of get-the-hell-out-of-my-face instinctive reaction. For that reason, I kept chucking that spinner into that fat trout's face in the hope it would eventually get pissed off enough to strike. And it did!

When that hog pounded on that spinner, it sent a jolt up my arm, and I knew: *Fish on!* That fish took line off my tiny Penn reel like there was no drag at all. However, I dared not increase the drag because the reel was only rigged with two-pound test line—I would have to finesse this fish to the net.

As rainbows do when hooked, that monster leaped from the water repeatedly, shaking its head, trying to throw the hook. It tore up that pool and put the other fish down. It made eleven all-out upstream runs against the current, but each time, I got him "back on the reel." Finally, I had exhausted him enough to get him in the landing net, and I had no intention of releasing him. Gabby and I would have a fine in-camp meal from that catch. I had won the battle. Persistence pays.

To "reduce a trout to possession" humanely, you "priest" it over the head. A priest is a small club, usually made of brass, used to rap the fish on the head between the eyes to shock its brain. On priesting a trout, its body goes suddenly rigid or quivers slightly, and then quickly goes limp. While that might seem cruel to the uninitiated, it is far more humane than simply placing the fish in a creel where it will suffocate slowly. Only I didn't have a priest with me. Mine stays on my fly fishing vest, and I was just out in the woods with a cheap six-piece backpacking rod and a plastic box full of spinners.

I scanned the ground for a suitable stick to substitute for my priest. I whacked that fish hard on the head. But to my utter amazement, it went nuts in the net, and I almost lost it! I threw the net and fish up the grassy hill, away from the water's edge. No way was I going to lose that fish to the water after a five-minute battle to land him after setting the hook, not to mention the almost two hours I spent casting to him!

I took off up the bank but fell over backward and tumbled down the hill into the water. My legs were numb and tingling from having been crouched down for more than two hours straight, and they just didn't work! I was covered in mud from asshole to shoe sole and more determined than ever to retrieve my catch.

When I regained my legs, I climbed up the bank, located my catch, and I whacked the fish once more. But it still kept squirming and managed to free itself from the net. I then had to act quickly to keep it from sliding down the grassy bank, back into the stream, where—even though it would no doubt die from the experience—it would be lost to me and wasted. I grabbed at it repeatedly but couldn't get a firm hold because it was slimy and writhing. It wasn't willing to give up, but neither was I. Finally, I got my boot on it and took my knife and pierced its skull through to its brain. It was then flaccid and ready for the creel.

The creel I had was one of the cheap Woodstream-brand vinyl kind with a twelve-inch ruler silkscreened on its side. It was good enough for my mobile fishing adventures on the bike but not very adequate for hard use. That creel was about thirteen or fourteen inches across. Only when I tried to place my catch into that tiny container did I come to realize the sheer size of it. It wouldn't fit!

To gauge the size of that beast, I laid it out flat alongside my rod. It measured from the butt of the rod up to the wrapping on the first guide, which I could later measure when I had a tape on hand (I later determined that fish had been twenty-two and a half inches long). I suddenly realized I had caught the largest stream-run trout of my entire trout-fishing life! I then had to get it back to camp and on ice, else risk wasting that magnificent fish.

I stuffed the fish in the creel with the tail sticking out one end and the head out the other. I scrambled quickly back through the woods to the bike. By that time, the temperature had risen into the eighties from the cool morning fifties back in camp. But in the interest of time, I kept my waders and wading boots on, which would make for a warm, sweaty ride back to Kemp's. I loaded all my gear on the bike as quickly as I could, but I saw no way to secure my catch without a bungee net or cord of any kind, all of which had been left back at camp.

So I slung the creel over my shoulder and rolled out with my catch blowing in the wind. I must have made for an interesting scene as I rolled down the hill into Keystone because I managed to draw a lot of stares from other riders as they spied me in waders, riding my bike with studded wading boots, and this fish head and tail projecting from under my armpit!

When I rolled up to the campground, I stopped at the owner's house just past the gate. The owner, Bruce, was sitting on the porch as I approached.

I asked, "Bruce, can you spare some butter?"

"What for?"

"This!"

I held up the overloaded creel.

Bruce smiled and said, "Just a sec…"

He went into the house and returned momentarily. When he did, he yelled, "Here you go!" before throwing a whole stick of butter my way.

"What do I owe you?"

He waved me off with a hearty "Get outta here!"

I jumped back on the bike and pulled up to our site. I noticed that the right-side saddlebag for Gabby's bike was sitting on the picnic table, but he and his bike were gone. That was a good sign. Gabby likely had been wrenching on his bike and gotten it fixed.

A couple had just arrived in the site next to ours, and they were making camp. I noticed they had a full-sized Coleman cooler that was empty.

"Hey, if I fill your cooler with ice, would you let me keep this fish in it?" I asked.

"You bet" is all the guy said.

I made three trips to the office for ice and completely covered the fish, leaving room for whatever the couple might want to add. The pressure was off—the fish was on ice and wouldn't spoil. I had had a perfect morning.

Not five minutes after I had iced down the fish, up rolled Gabby with a huge grin on his face. His morning was quite interesting too. He managed to get a ride to the Harley dealer where he bought the parts needed to heal his FLT. He was actually coming back from a test ride when he rolled up. He fixed that bike in the campground with the limited tools he carried on the bike. He's a damn good wrench.

"Man, you weren't kidding! That Spearfish Canyon is awesome!" Gabby proclaimed.

"I told you that you would like the Hills. But remember, it only gets better from here."

"No way! That'd be hard to beat. I'm gonna do that run again in the other direction."

I completely understood. It had been years since my first run through the Hills, but I could remember as clearly as yesterday the sense of awe I had looking at the jaw-dropping sights along the way the first time I came to the Black Hills Motor Classic (the Sturgis Rally). I was glad to be able to share that with my friend.

I said, "Okay, I'll go with you back through the Canyon, but whatya say we get something to eat first?"

"Sure, whatya have in mind?"

I walked over to the neighboring site, reached into the cooler, and slowly withdrew my morning's prize.

Gabby's jaw dropped.

"You caught *that*!" he asked.

"Sure did. Now let's eat."

I cleared the picnic table under the shelter and got out my little Coleman one-burner stove and folding-handle frying pan. Each time I went back and forth to my gear bag, I would duck to avoid banging my head on the too-low table shelter.

That fish was so big that even after I cut off the head and tail, I still had to cut it in thirds to cook it all in the pan. I used the whole stick of butter that Bruce had donated, and we ate the entire fish between us. There's nothing better than fresh-caught fish in camp.

As I was finished cooking the first third, I called over to Gabby to bring the metal plates from my gear bag and the salt and pepper too. Gabby was eager to eat and came to the table full speed ahead.

Before I could yell out a warning, *wham*! Gabby walked right into the lower edge of the shelter on his way to the table. His eyes went crossed, and he reeled back and almost to his knees. That had to hurt!

Now, I haven't quite figured out just exactly what evil demons I have within me, but I get an awful lot of amusement from *other peoples'* pain, possibly through watching too much Three Stooges as a kid. I flat out roared laughing! Gabby didn't share in the humor but instead spent the next five minutes cussing me and the shelter equally. That of course only made me laugh harder!

Now, don't get me wrong—I'm not a completely uncompassionate prick. It wasn't like I hadn't warned him in the dark the night before as we set up camp. And besides, I figured I sort of earned the right to laugh—I had done the very thing two years before and almost blacked out.

So when Gabby single-handedly tried to relocate the picnic table shelter with his skull, I *had* to laugh…what're friends for!

WHAT'RE FRIENDS FOR? (PART 4)

The Wallet Run—Gabby Pays Me Back...

To say that Gabby has his quirks would be an understatement. To *only* mention Gabby's quirks would be unfair—I've got my share too. They say if you really want to know someone, go travel with them. We would find out just how true that was into week two of our trip.

I suppose my quirk that annoyed Gabby most was my compulsive desire to make miles—that is, once in the saddle, keep rolling until you make your destination. While I have mellowed over the years and now slow down to suck in the scenery, that just wasn't me back in 2000. If I had an itinerary, I would stick to it. Gabby would complain that I wouldn't even take time out for a piss break. "Iron Kidneys," he eventually named me. That behavior was just in keeping with Iron Butt thinking—in other words, do all things at one time when you stop for gas, like grab a drink, use the bathroom, and so on. It all made perfect sense to me, but apparently not everyone can run from tankful to tankful like I prefer. Gabby had actually explored getting a catheter so that he could relieve himself while following me down the road on our long runs. I pitied the driver who tailgated Gabby!

Gabby's quirk that most annoyed me was his compulsive set-in-his-ways routines. For example, Gabby *will* have his coffee in the morning and no matter how long it delays us from getting an early start (remember the reason he broke down in the Badlands?). And, on checking into a motel, he would "move in"—in other words, he would compulsively put underwear in the "underwear" drawer, socks in the "sock" drawer, and so on, which to me was a complete waste of time when you're checking out the very next morning. Just live out of your saddlebags, for shit sakes!

Neither one of our styles is "right" nor "wrong," but the differences sure make for some amusing time on the road. And so while Gabby's style resulted in him getting stranded in the Badlands, sooner or later, my style would bite me in the ass too. Only I didn't know it would be the day after we left Jackson Hole.

On leaving Jackson Hole, our destination was Moab, Utah, a former uranium mining town that today makes its money from recreational tourism—mostly mountain biking and four-wheel driving tours into the slick rock back country and float trips on the Colorado River. Moab is just over 500 miles from Jackson if you take the shortest route. In 2000, however, there were wildfires raging all over the West that necessitated some lengthy detours. By the time we made Moab late that afternoon, we had logged an additional 125 miles of detours. One detour alone took us 70 miles out of our way. Ordinarily, added miles didn't bother us—it was just more riding time. But that day was annoying because of the weather extremes between Jackson and Moab.

The heat and single-digit humidity that contributed to so many wildfires that year also took its toll on us. Air-cooled Harley engines put more heat on the rider as the ambient temperature rises. When we left the Super Slab to jump on US 191, I noticed the temperature at Cruel Jack's truck stop was ninety-eight. That made for a hot ride over the high desert into Moab.

Counter to my characteristic tankful-to-tankful whipping-and-driving riding style, I took plenty of time out at each fuel stop to take on water and find restful shade. About 100 miles out of Moab, we fueled up for the last time before arriving in town, and I discussed the evening's and next day's plans with Gabby as we hid in the shade of the gas station in the treeless desert.

Due to the fire detours, we had already clocked 500-plus miles with 100 or so more to go before finding our motel for the night, and we were both worn out from the heat.

"Man, you told me time and time again before we left that we'd be doing 500-plus-mile days, but I guess it just didn't sink in!" exclaimed Gabby. "I'm beat."

"Well, don't worry. Tomorrow is only about 350 miles to Kanab," I said.

"Great, I'll be sleeping in."

"Well, we really should get on the road early. It's monsoon season all over the desert southwest, and we don't want to get stuck in any thunderstorms. They blow up later in the heat of the afternoon and can be fierce, with plenty of lightning. And besides, the earlier we leave, the cooler our ride will be."

Gabby said, "We'll have to see about that, but what's the plan from here?"

"Well, thanks to all of the 35-mile-per-hour detours, it's too late to hit Arches National Park. And it's just too damn hot out now, anyway."

"We came all this way, and you want to skip it!"

"I've seen it all before. But if you want to peel off and ride through the park, I'll meet you in Moab at the motel, and then we'll grab dinner."

Gabby seemed a bit disappointed and said, "Nah, that's okay. I'll roll on with you."

We left Jackson Hole at 7:00 a.m. while it was just 35 degrees out. On arriving in Moab at 5:30 p.m., it was 105, down from a high of 109. I have no idea what the temperature climbed to out in the desert on the way to Moab, but I knew I wanted to get off the desert the next day as early as possible. Riding in that kind of heat is no fun at all.

We checked into the motel and offloaded our bikes. I just tossed my white-water gear bags onto one of the beds, but Gabby started to unpack and organize his clothes in the dresser. I went ballistic.

"Are you kidding me!" I yelled.

"What!" Gabby snapped back.

"We're leaving first thing in the morning. We've been baking our brains out in the heat all day. I'm tired and thirsty—I'm going to dinner! And what the hell do you need to move in for, anyway?"

Gabby just shrugged his shoulders and said nothing while continuing to unpack.

The heat made us both irritable—all the more reason to eat and get refreshed before settling into the room. I told Gabby how to get to the steakhouse where I was headed and walked out for dinner.

Shortly after, Gabby joined me, and we ate a great meal and both drank probably a gallon of iced tea each. The desert heat had sucked the life from us, and we had gotten dehydrated without realizing it—despite drinking water along our route all day. And it wore on our nerves.

We went back to our room after dinner, and to my surprise, Gabby had almost everything he packed for the trip spread out in the room before he followed me to dinner. He was still intent on "moving in." I said nothing; I was disgusted. Not only was that a huge waste of time before he could settle in and get rested, he would waste as much time in the morning repacking his bike. The unstoppable force had met the immovable object—we both would do what we wanted. And that was that.

I just shook my head at Gabby and put the contents of my riding vest and jeans in the nightstand drawer, undressed, set an alarm, and went off to sleep. Gabby had me so flustered that I failed to stick to one of my nightly routines, and that deviation would cost me dearly the next day.

The alarm went off as scheduled, but I was already awake. I threw a pillow at Gabby to wake him, but the only response I got was, "You prick!"

I tried to get him up a couple of times, but when he didn't stir, I just started to pack my bike instead. Because I only had to put my clothes into one of the three bags I carried on the trip and strap the bags on the bike, I was ready in no time.

"Gabby, let's go. We don't want to get caught in the valley in a thunderstorm [Monument Valley] or ride in the heat of the day again."

"What about breakfast? I gotta have my coffee."

"Breakfast? The last thing we did before hitting the sack was eat a huge meal. You can't be hungry already!"

"I'm not rolling out without my coffee!"

"Well, I'm not waiting that long. I'll ride slowly, and you can catch me along the route. You have the motel information in the itinerary I gave you in case we don't hook back up until Kanab. Be safe."

And with that, I rolled out of town. I was so annoyed he didn't stick to our plan that I didn't even gas up in Moab. I just jumped on the bike and started to make miles.

As you leave Moab toward the south, you eventually come into some high country with nice sweeping curves, which make for pleasant riding. Despite telling Gabby I would roll on slowly, I couldn't resist the temptation to twist the wrist and blast through the curvy stuff. On one curve, which had no cautionary speed marking, I nearly went off the road all the way to the left lane fog line where there was no guardrail—just a two hundred-foot drop-off. If there had been an oncoming car around that turn or just a bit of oil, sand, or gravel at the edge of that road, I would have gone over the cliff, and Gabby would never have found me. That was a close one! After that sphincter-pucker near miss, I kept my speed down.

About sixty-five miles out of Moab, I had to switch to reserve because I hadn't filled up before leaving. No problem—Blanding was just ten miles farther up the road.

I pulled into the first gas station, and as I dismounted my bike and reached for my back pocket for my wallet, I suddenly realized, *Oh shit! My wallets are in the nightstand back at the motel in Moab!*

I moved my bike from the gas pumps and frantically grabbed the phone book in the phone booth to get the number for the motel. While I had no cash or credit card, I did have a calling card in one of my saddlebags. I explained the situation to the woman who had checked us in the night before.

She said, "Oh your friend just left here with your wallets! I told him to leave them behind in case you remembered and came back."

That wouldn't have helped. I didn't have enough gas in the bike to make it back to Moab and no cash on hand to buy more. I was stranded in Blanding, Utah, and had no choice but to wait for Gabby to roll into town with my wallets.

That was my own fault. I had let Gabby get to me the night before with his whole "moving in" routine, such that I failed to adhere to one of my own on-the-road routines that I followed religiously to avoid just such a problem. Instead of putting my stuff in the night-stand like I had done the night before, I would always put my bike key, pocketknife, and both wallets into one of my boots. That way, in the morning when putting on my boots, there'd be no way I could forget anything important before checking out of the room. What's worse, I always carried a second wallet tethered around my neck with $1,000 in $100 bills and another $1,000 in traveler's checks, and a second credit card, plus my spare bike key, just in case I lost my primary wallet. But the backup was left along with my primary.

I'm an idiot! I thought.

Possibly the only more impatient person than Gabby is me. Waiting for him to roll into Blanding was going to test my nerves, especially because if he had only just left the motel and hadn't yet gotten his coffee and breakfast, I would be waiting a good two hours or more before he would make Blanding. Blanding is a Mormon town, and that was Sunday—in other words, no place to go and nothing to do but sit on the curb and keep an eye and ear out for Gabby to roll through.

It took me about an hour and a half to get to Blanding. I figured that if Gabby went to the slowest café in Moab, he would arrive in Blanding within two and a half hours. I parked my bike along the curb at the edge of town and sat alongside it to wait. My bike was unmistakable—a green and black FLH with three yellow and black Sealine rafting bags strapped to it. No way could Gabby miss me on his way into town. I just had to wait until he arrived.

When two and a half hours had passed, I was anxious. When three and a half hours had passed with no sign of Gabby, I was worried. Gabby is an even more aggressive rider than I—what if he hit that same unmarked turn where I had my close call, only he didn't recover from it? That was a grisly thought, but how else might I explain why an hour and a half ride from Moab could possibly take more than three and a half hours, even with coffee and breakfast thrown in?

There *could* be some less gruesome explanation why he hadn't caught up—possibly his charging system quit again, and he was stranded between Moab and Blanding. Nevertheless, I then had to think about my safety and getting to Kanab where we had a room reserved for the night.

I had my Palm Pilot organizer on the bike, which contained all of the motel phone numbers and confirmation numbers where we had reservations along our planned route, as well as personal identifying information and credit card numbers.

Armed with only the Palm Pilot info, I walked into every open business in Blanding, which on a Sunday—in any Mormon town—was limited to C-stores and gas stations. I asked each clerk whether they could give me $50 in cash, charged against my credit card, based only on a number I provided and without any photo ID.

"Yeah, right, scooter trash!" their looks seemed to convey as one store clerk after another denied my request.

I went through every gas station along the main drag through town. Finally, in the last one, the clerk said she worked in a bank during the week and had a way to verify me. She said I would have to call someone I knew, and then have that person call her and describe me to her and provide some additional identifying information. My luck was with me—my girlfriend Stacey was actually home on a Sunday afternoon and made the call.

Under the circumstances, the clerk could only give me $35 on my card, but that would give me enough gas money to get to Kanab, 280 miles away, and enough for some food if Gabby didn't catch up to me before then. I was set.

It was then around 1:00 p.m., and there still was no sign of Gabby. Nevertheless, I was obligated to wait by my bike in case he would be along momentarily. I walked the half mile or so back to my bike and sat on the curb and waited. And waited. And waited some more.

It was then 3:00 p.m., and the temp had climbed into the upper nineties. That was exactly what I had hoped to avoid by getting on the road early. Where the hell was he!

Something *must* have happened. There's no way Gabby could have rolled through town and missed my bike while I was in the gas stations trying to get a cash advance...or could he? Might he now be *ahead* of me?

In the grand scheme of things, I couldn't complain; my luck was not that bad. Sure, I had stranded myself because I let Gabby's quirks rattle my nerves and throw me off of my routine, but sitting on the curb in Blanding afforded me an awesome view of the red rock desert with blue sky above for as far as the eye could see. But my luck was about to change.

As I sat there in the oppressive heat, a gentle breeze began to stir and then *splat!* Some friggin' bird cut loose its load, and it landed on my left shoulder—or so I thought initially. I looked up but saw no offending bird in sight. Then another *splat* hit home. It was starting to rain those huge drops that are the precursor to the high desert afternoon thunderstorms.

Despite the blue sky in front of me, I looked up and back to see my black cloud directly overhead and a blue-black sky as dark as night rolling in over me. The drops increased in size and frequency. I had less than a minute to dig my rain gear out of the bike and suit up before the heavens opened wide. Then came the lightning and deafening thunder.

It was pouring then—a full-on monsoon cloudburst. These can last for as little as a few minutes or turn into an all-out lingering gully-washer, complete with flash flooding that can be fatal in the desert if the lightning doesn't blast you from your bike first.

I got on my bike and pulled back into the gas station to fuel up and dodge at least some of the rain. Still no sign of Gabby.

It was then 4:00 p.m. Gabby or no Gabby, I had to get on the road. As much as I had wanted to avoid the desert heat and monsoon rains by getting on the road early, I wanted more to avoid heavy rain after dark.

It was a cold rain, and it pressed the Gore-Tex jacket against my arms and shoulders. By the time I made it to the other end of Blanding, the last bank thermometer in town indicated just seventy-two degrees or a twenty-six degree drop in just ten minutes since the storm began.

The storm was impressive with awesome lightning everywhere and earsplitting thunder. While storms of such intensity don't usually last, that one did. I navigated through sideways wind and rain and even occasional dime-sized hail for over one hundred miles before it let up. When it did, I stopped at a Navajo tribal store to add my sweatshirt under my rain gear. It was just sixty-five degrees then, and I was getting cold. Ironically, I *did* beat the desert heat but not the way I had planned!

Riding through Monument Valley Navajo Tribal Park provides incredible scenery. Even if you have seen Monument Valley through your wide-screen high-definition TV in some documentary, you won't believe your eyes on seeing it in person.

Unfortunately for me, "seeing" it on that trip was not in the cards—the storm had regained its strength and made for a very challenging ride. Much of the two-lane road in the Valley is completely shoulder-less—the asphalt ends within an inch of the fog line. There is no room for error on the curves and hills, and the road is not well-maintained on the reservation. There are deep ruts from the weight of the vehicles that channel the water into several-inch-deep gullies that can cause instant hydroplaning, which is especially dangerous on a two-wheeler. That was exactly the sort of ride I wanted to avoid and would have if I hadn't left my stuff in the nightstand the night before! I was pissed off—*really* pissed off—at myself.

Despite the unplanned stay over in Blanding, I was still on track to make Kanab before dark. I would have too until I came across a flash-flooded section of road where the water was a raging torrent—no way would I attempt to cross even though I had ridden through foot-deep still-water flooded roads in the past. The current can bring disaster quickly. There was nothing I could do but wait it out.

Fortunately, flash floods are just that—they come *and* go in a flash. Once the worst of the rains had subsided, the flooded road drained quickly. In just forty minutes, the road was passable again although not easily. The flooding had deposited a heavy layer of mud across about four hundred yards of road. While the narrow bike tires cut through the layer down to the hard road, the bike squirmed quite a bit even though I never went over thirty miles an hour through that stretch.

It was then getting dark, and I had about one hundred miles left to Kanab. It was still raining but without the intensity it had for the last few hours. I gassed up one more time and hung around the station, trying to get warm and hoping the rain would blow through. I was not eager to get back on the bike because besides riding now at night in heavy rain, I would face the added hazard of riding through heavy deer and elk country. In about a half hour, the rain did let up a bit, but it just wouldn't stop. Nevertheless, it was time to press on.

I reluctantly mounted my bike, thumbed the starter, and headed out. That last stretch would prove to be the worst. About thirty miles out of Kanab, the road was under construction. The asphalt had been stripped, and I was driving on the compacted roadbed. As anyone knows who has ever driven on the rock-hard desert, that same surface will turn to a gel from a soaking rain, and you can easily slide off the shoulder of the road where your tire treads fill with mud and you have no steering response. And while the roadbed had been compacted, it was still made of the local soil and prone to "floating" when wet.

I hit several of these floated soft spots at only thirty-five to forty miles an hour, and the ass end of the bike started to come around. I was not in control at all. I only kept the bike up because the soft spots didn't go on for too long—that is, traction was suddenly restored, and the bike righted itself after skating over these "gel holes." If any of those had been longer, I would surely have laid the bike down.

It was so dark out that I couldn't distinguish the road from the black horizon through the raindrops on my face shield. Several times I reached for the brakes as a tumble weed blew across my path. If any had been deer, I wouldn't have been able to stop in time anyway. I was riding through an ink-black night on a gel-covered road in the rain with little visibility, trusting solely on Providence to get me to Kanab in one piece.

About five miles from Kanab, I was back on hard road, and the rain had tapered off to a sprinkle. It was time to get off the road and grab a bite as soon as I hit town.

I remembered telling Gabby that if he and I ever made it to Kanab, we would have to eat at Houston's Trails End restaurant. That café-diner has the best home-cooked meals in town.

By the time I made Houston's, the rain had stopped. I parked my bike sideways—to give a profile view—in case Gabby happened to roll by, which at that hour seemed unlikely.

I went in and slumped into a booth, completely exhausted from the white-knuckle ride over the desert, and I was starving. I checked on my remaining funds from the $35 starting stake and would have enough, plus tip, for a good hot meal.

After the waitress took my order, I peeled off my rain gear, just glad to be in town in one piece. I settled back into the booth, and the tension started to drain from my neck and shoulders. As I got up from the table to go to the salad bar, Gabby walked in the door!

He spied me as he came around the corner and—with a shit-eating grin on his face—bellowed at the top of his lungs, "YOU FORGET SOMETHING?"

He was holding both of my wallets in his left hand! Man, I was happy to see them and relieved he was alive. I told him so.

Gabby said, "Yeah, well the 'alive' part might not have been just twenty miles from here!"

I assumed he meant the snot-slick construction zone, which I knew all too well.

Suddenly, I realized he wasn't wearing any rain gear.

"Hey, wait a minute. Where're you coming from?" I asked.

He had taken the exact same route as I had.

"Didn't you hit rain?"

"No, but there was one helluva a storm ahead of me most of the way."

"What? You never got wet?"

"Not a drop. It was wet everywhere I rode since about Monument Valley, but I never got rained on."

"You lucky son of a bitch! You know what I've been through today, waiting for you to catch up!"

I went on to explain how I was stranded without my wallets and how long I waited for him to catch up. And then it hit me: he was only five minutes behind me at Houston's. It didn't add up, and I asked him what took him so long to follow me.

Gabby explained that since he had come all that way, he decided to head *back north* after breakfast and film Arches National Park.

"What! You knew I was stranded with no cash or credit cards and you *headed north*! And what do you mean 'filming'?"

He chuckled and said, "I brought my camcorder along. Figured I get some nice scenic shots."

"How often did you stop to shoot video while I was parked alongside the road?"

"Oh, I never stopped."

"Wait a minute," I said. "If you didn't stop, how did you record anything?"

"I just locked down the throttle screw tight and worked the camera."

"*What!* Are you friggin' nuts! You're right handed, so you held the camera with your throttle hand?"

"Yeah" was all he said with a smile.

"You know how dangerous that was? I'm starting to think I'm lucky to have ever gotten my wallets back at all!"

"Oh, you're lucky to get your wallets, all right, but not for that reason. I almost died back in that construction zone. I'm lucky to be here!"

"What, you slide on that gel mud?"

"I never hit anything like that [once the rain stops, the desert soil firms up fast]. After going up to Arches, I figured I'd have to make up time to catch up to you, so I flew through the desert. I passed *everyone*. About twenty miles out from here, I got behind a panel van and couldn't see too well ahead. I started to pass and saw lights, but they were way up the road. So I pulled around, but that guy was *flying*. Just as I was even with the driver's door on the van, I was stuck between it and the other car, which went wide to miss me.

The wind turbulence was so great my bike wobbled, and the mirror hit the van. I looked in my other mirror, and that's when I saw the lights come around and realized the other car had spun out of control and off the road. I looked back a second time, and that's when I saw the red flashing lights. It was a cop!"

"Holy shit! What happened next?"

"I just pulled over and waited. I was still shaking from hitting that van. Then the cop got out of his car and charged my way. The officer said, 'You ran me off the road, you son of a bitch!'

"I said, 'Officer, you can give me all the tickets you want, I'm just happy to be alive.'" Gabby went on. "Apparently, he called for backup because when he stomped off back to his car to write me up, I heard a Blazer tearing through the brush and saw its lights flashing. The driver was a lot younger officer than the guy I ran off the road.

"That officer said with a smile on his face, 'Man, what did you do to him? He's really pissed.'

"I explained what happened, and he laughed. Then he told me I was in a no-passing zone. I never saw any signs, but they were there—just down in the ditch where you can't see them.

"He said, 'You coming from Sturgis?'

"Yes, sir.

"'Heading up to Grand Canyon?'

"Yes, sir.

"Then he said, 'Well, you seem okay to me. Here's what you do: tomorrow, first thing, go to the courthouse and pay your fines. If you do that, the tickets will never show up on your license back home.'

"I said, 'Thanks!'"

Gabby earned three tickets for running that cop off the road: (1) speeding, (2) unsafe passing, and (3) passing in a "no passing" zone.

So I asked, "Did you get it on video?"

He just shot me a look, and I knew what he would say next.

"Prick!"

We left Houston's and got to our motel. Unlike the night before, where Gabby moved into the room, on that night he didn't unpack anything but his shaving kit. I busted out laughing; I knew why.

I said, "Oh, you see how you are—tomorrow, you'll be up bright and early to head to the courthouse. Breakfast and coffee be damned!"

He replied, "Damn right! Those three tickets show up on my license, I lose my CDL."

"Well, we're only seventy-seven miles from the North Rim. We have *all day* to make it to our cabin for the night. I was thinking of sleeping in and maybe even having breakfast at the Rocking V after leaving this fine motel room at checkout time, around 11:00 a.m."

Gabby started to laugh then too and said, "You're a five-star prick, you know that?"

"Hey, I might as well be good at something..."

Back in our room, Gabby asked me three times whether I had set an alarm for the morning (I had), but I never gave him a straight answer. I just said, "Good night."

I had to have my fun at his expense, which, in a way, was sort of due. After all, he kept me waiting in the desert while he went to Arches, all the while knowing he had my wallets.

The next morning, Gabby was up before me *and* had his bike packed. I cracked up and started in on him some more.

"Hey, Gabby, do you even know *where* the county courthouse is located?"

A panicked look swept over him, and he said, "What! You mean it's not in Kanab?"

"Well, all I know is, it's in the county seat."

I knew full well where the courthouse was located—it was just two blocks down from our motel, in easy walking distance. I didn't drag out his torture much longer.

"Follow me," I said through my suppressed laughter.

"But these tickets have to be paid first thing or—"

"They will be."

He didn't say another word as I walked us to the courthouse. We arrived five minutes before business hours. The minute someone unlocked the door, Gabby found the clerk, signed for his admission of guilt, and coughed up the cash to protect his CDL.

When Gabby emerged from the courthouse, I said, "Hey, break-fast is on me—I never thanked you for having my back and getting my wallets to me."

"Gee, thanks, but come to think of it, I never thanked you for having my back in the Badlands after I cooked my charging system."

Yeah, Gabby, you did, maybe without the words but by having *my* back when I screwed up as a result of my impatience and that we *both* rag on each other when it's each other's turn in the hot seat—and without getting mad. That's thanks enough.

And if you ask me, *that's* what friends are for!

PARTY AT HEELS'S

Our friend, Paul, knew lots of people through the computer long before Facebook or Twitter existed. Back then, everything was a "blog" or internet bulletin board (IBB), through which like-minded people connected.

It was through some biker IBB that Paul met and later introduced me to "BlackHeels4You," or just Heels for short.

Heels lived in a centuries-old stone farmhouse outside of York, Pennsylvania, on the side of some wooded mountain. She was a pretty cool biker and generously hosted a great party at her property every September to coincide with the annual Harley-Davidson York factory open house.

Biker friends from the IBB came from all over the Northeast and Midwest to attend Heels's party. Although her property was mostly covered in hardwood forest, there were several meadows that had been cleared a hundred years or more before, which Heels would bushhog just before the party so we could all camp out on the property.

Paul was the ringleader for most of the best stuff that transpired during those parties, and he liked his privacy—sort of. In order to avoid people cutting through our private side parties, Paul would always arrive early on Friday to claim the uppermost meadow for our group. I could never get away until Saturday, except the year I got my '99 Wide Glide, but I always managed to find a spot to park my bike and pitch my tent on reaching the upper meadow.

In 1999, I was able to head out on Friday. When I got to the upper meadow, no one was there. I was sure I had heard Paul was planning on making the Open House party, but no one was in the upper meadow at all. So I rode back down the rocky footpath and pitched camp across from another tent in a wide spot along the path—no sense in claiming a whole meadow when I couldn't be sure who from our chapter might show up. And if our chapter did show up, I could always move my camp up the hill on Saturday.

I partied at the house until about midnight before turning in. It had been a long week at work, and I was beat. When I got back to my camp, everything was covered in dew, which is common back in those eastern mountains. I turned in and fell asleep immediately. I slept straight through the night except for some commotion that woke me about 3:00 a.m.—I assumed just more of Heels's guests making it back to their camp. On exiting my tent the next day, I discovered I was mistaken—not just any guests but some pranksters.

The first sound I heard on waking was "Damn! Look at *this* motherfucker. He can drink!"

I had no idea what that meant, but it came from the neighboring campsite across the path from mine. On crawling out of my tent, it became clear. All around my tent and especially near the entrance were strewn maybe forty to fifty empty beer cans. It looked like my site was occupied by someone with a serious drinking problem! Who the hell would have littered my camp like that! I picked up the site as best I could and set out to haul all the empty cans in my saddlebags, down to the rubbish bin at the house. There were so many of them I had to make two trips.

I carried the cans to my bike, and on seeing it, I was furious! Someone had stuck marshmallows all over the brand-new windshield and the gas tank, glued in place with the aid of the dew. It took me a half hour to clean most of that sugary gunk off the bike just to make my trash runs down to the house.

This was taken after most of the cans had been taken to the trash. The marshmallow residue was still visible on the windshield!

I was certain the 3:00 a.m. commotion was caused by whoever pulled these two pranks, and I was out for revenge. I swore I would find out who had done that before the weekend was out and get even.

I spent the day at the York factory test driving all the new 2000 Harleys and perusing the vendor tents. Although I ate breakfast and lunch at the Open House, Heels was cooking an entire pig back at her place for dinner, and I was eager to get back before dark and join the party.

On returning to Heels's, there sat Paul, along with Tony and Diane—fellow Rogue Hog members. They had arrived the night before, only very late, and they occupied the upper meadow. After we all ate and drank to excess, I broke my camp along the footpath and settled in with Paul and the rest of our chapter up in the meadow, where we always started our own private parties.

While I was making camp, I told Paul, Diane, and Tony what happened to me the night before. They were all quite sympathetic... at first.

We'd all had our share of beer at the barbecue, and while one hundred-pound Diane could outdrink me and Paul, she couldn't hide anything while drunk. She started laughing hysterically while

I told them the first thing I had heard on waking in my tent that morning.

Turns out the culprits were Paul, Tony, and Diane! While making their way to the upper meadow, they recognized my tent and new bike and scoured the party area for empty beer cans to litter my site with and for me to crawl over on leaving my tent. And it was Diane's idea to glue the marshmallows to my windshield and tank. On learning these pranks were pulled by my chapter cohorts, all I could do was laugh—along with the three perpetrators!

SOME OF PAUL'S ANTICS

Besides my friend Gabby, we have a mutual friend—Paul, who has generated lots of laughs for us over the years.

Anyway, this past summer (2019), I joined up with Paul, who was hosting biker friends in from Germany—Werner and Doris. We met at Wild Bill's campground up in the Black Hills during the Sturgis Rally. One night, we met with some of Werner's German friends, who now live in LA. We were swapping stories and had a few laughs from everyone at Werner's friends' campsite, but the most laughs came while I was telling "Paul" stories. If you think I had a guardian angel on two wheels after my near-death motorcycle crashes, you should have ridden with Paul back in our Rogue Hog days!

Back then, Paul was riding "Protector"—a 1977 seventy-four-inch Shovelhead FLH. For some reason, Paul got it in his head to add an inline fuel filter to the bike in the line from the tank to the carburetor fuel bowl. That worked okay but only while he had at least a half tank of fuel. Below that, there wasn't enough static head pressure for the fuel to pass through the restrictive filter easily, and the bike would sometimes break up and lose speed as it was starved for gas.

Quick-thinking Paul would remove one of the fuel filler caps— *lit cigarette in hand*—lean forward, and then blow into the tank to force fuel through the line again while traveling at highway speeds. It worked!

We all just shook our heads as he was our Road Captain on most runs back then. One year, as he was leading a bunch of us on the Run to the Wall in Washington DC over Memorial Day weekend, we were hauling ass in the left lane of I-95 when suddenly Protector started losing speed. Paul quickly removed a fuel cap and proceeded to pressurize the tank. Only that time, he drifted off the road down the grassy embankment in the median but never missed a beat—he kept blowing into the tank, probably unaware that he'd left the roadway!

There was a large interstate sign in the median, and Paul was headed straight toward it. In his leaned over position, Paul *just* cleared the bottom edge of the sign, unaware that it was even there. He got the fuel flow restarted and sat upright just as Protector cleared the sign. Paul then nonchalantly throttled the bike back up to the roadway and proceeded to lead us to the Wall. He had no idea how close he had come to being decapitated that day until we filled him in later. Soon after, he removed the auxiliary filter from Protector!

Paul is a pothead. He's been one since his marine corps days back during the Vietnam War. Sometimes, Paul would smoke while leading a group of bikes on our chapter runs. On one such trip, my bike was the second one in our line. While we always rode staggered formation, we would end up side-by-side when stopped in traffic.

I once smelled the unmistakable odor of pot when I rolled up next to Paul at a light in a small town—and so could the cops in the left lane who rolled up next to us! The officers were eyeing Paul intently—they were sure it was Paul who had blazed the joint they smelled.

But Paul was aware of his surroundings, and just as the cruiser was almost even with Paul, I saw him suck the lit joint into his mouth by curling it in on his tongue. Nothing to see here, officer!

I saw everything and about died laughing. The passenger-side officer never took his eyes off Paul but never did anything either, even when Paul coughed smoke through his nose!

When the light turned green, Paul clutched Protector, slammed first gear, whacked the throttle, then feathered the clutch, and pulled away very slowly. Well, on hearing Paul rev his bike, the driver of the cruiser mashed the gas, probably figuring he'd keep up with—and keep eyes on—Paul. But because Paul barely inched forward, the cruiser shot passed us, giving Paul time to spit out the still-lit joint before rolling casually by the cruiser that had slowed down to watch us. Paul waved and smiled as he led our group past the officers.

I laughed for the next three miles!

PAYBACK

Back in 2000, I persuaded my good friend Gabby to join me on an Iron Butt run to Sturgis and beyond. An Iron Butt requires minimally that you log at least one thousand miles in the saddle in twenty-four hours or less. We did that easily in about twenty-one hours the first day of our trip.

Anyway, Gabby and I don't see eye-to-eye on what to pack when we go on the road. Sure, we're in sync where it comes to taking tools, rain gear, and the like, but we part ways where it comes to taking fishing gear (me) or *an espresso machine* (Gabby)!

I told flatlander Gabby to be prepared for extremes of weather in my neck of the woods. For example, it could be over a hundred degrees across the high plains, down to the fifties or even forties going over the Beartooth Mountains, so I told him to be sure to bring layers. He didn't listen to me. Instead, he brought a light riding jacket and his electrically heated Gerbing jacket liner, whereas I had a lined wool sweater, hooded sweatshirt jacket, heavy lined canvas shirts, and my leather chaps and heavy leather riding jacket for the cooler temps and light, white long-sleeve cotton shirts for the hot regions.

On learning that Gabby didn't have *anything but* the Gerbing heated liner, I said to him, "You're gonna regret not having layers if you blow the fuse for that thing!"

Gabby laughed it off, and off we went.

After about a week and a half—and several Sturgis misadventures later—we made our way to Jackson Hole, Wyoming. I think we literally got the last available motel room in all of Jackson that night, and we paid a premium price for it too.

The next day was cold in Jackson when we rolled out—just thirty-five degrees. I put on my leathers and even put on my helmet for warmth. It only got colder on down through Hoback Junction. I eventually pulled over to put on all my layers. Gabby thought that was funny. He was toasty warm with the Gerbing thermostat dialed all the way up, and he made sure I knew it.

The added layers helped. But we were riding in the shade of the mountains, and it was colder than in Jackson. Eventually, I got that bone-chill cold and was shakin' like a dog shittin' razor blades, much to Gabby's amusement. I knew because he would ride up alongside me and unzip the collar of his jacket and fan himself, like he was too hot, while laughing the whole time—the prick!

Even when we had gotten close to the interstate and the temperature had risen to eighty, I kept some of my layers on—especially the black leathers—to absorb the then-abundant sunshine.

Before we jumped on the Super Slab, Gabby waved me to the side of the road to say we should stop someplace for breakfast. He added, "Make sure it's someplace with air conditioning!" before almost falling out of the saddle from laughter—prick!

I never fully shook off that cold until 5:30 p.m. that day when we were headed into Moab, Utah, where it had *cooled down to* 105 degrees.

Five months later, in the dead of winter, Gabby and I were riding in the mountains of West Virginia. That time, with the addition of two layers of Merino wool long johns to everything I had on the morning we left Jackson, I stayed warm. Gabby still only had his riding jacket and heated Gerbing liner, plus the heated Gerbing gloves, pants, and socks, all of which kept him quite warm, despite the strain on his old bike's charging system.

The morning we left Seneca Rocks was quite chilly—low twenties. We decided to eat at a very out-of-the-way restaurant that we knew of that was about sixty miles from the Rocks. Not too far from the Rocks, however, Gabby flagged me over to the side of the road.

He was cold, and it showed. Apparently—*get this*—the fuse for the Gerbing gear blew! He didn't carry a spare—probably because it would take up too much room better used by his espresso machine!

He asked me to check my spare parts, which I did, and I reported back, "Sorry, I don't have any spare fuses."

A look of "Oh shit!" came over his face. I enjoyed that immensely, considering how he had taunted me back during our USA summer run and especially because I had said to him, "…regret not having layers if you blow the fuse…" when I noticed he wasn't packing layers.

So we mounted the bikes and rode the next fifty miles or so to breakfast. I was sure it would warm up the longer the sun was up, but the stubborn mountain air didn't change much by the time we rolled up to the restaurant.

Gabby couldn't hide the fact that he was near frozen. When he dismounted his bike, he was so stiff he could barely bend his leg and almost fell off. He was in serious trouble—probably at the onset of hypothermia. Despite enjoying his misery for the last 60 miles, I had to come clean—no way could he make the next 220 miles safely back to his house without keeping warm.

We entered the restaurant and got a pot of hot coffee first thing. Gabby was shaking uncontrollably—kind of like I had been that morning out of Jackson.

I actually felt sorry for him at that point and said, "Let me go check my spare parts again. Maybe I missed something."

I went out to the bike and immediately retrieved the needed 7.5 amp fuse, which I knew I had all along.

On returning to our table, I held up the fuse and declared, "Found one!"

You would have thought I had just handed him a winning lottery ticket. He snatched it from my hands and bellowed, "Thanks!"

But by that point, I could hardly contain my laughter, and Gabby noticed.

He said, "You knew you had this the whole time, didn't you?"

"Yep! You remember when I froze my ass off leaving Jackson?"

In a low voice, he muttered, "Ain't this a bitch."

Then he got up and went out to his bike to install the replacement fuse. And I am certain that on the way out to his bike, he thought to himself about me, *Prick!*

Yes, Gabby, Karma's a bitch!

Bugs Are Bugs

Back in 2002, I took a southern route across country from the east coast to visit friends in Southern California. In Texas, Oklahoma, New Mexico, and Arizona, I mostly stayed on the old Route 66. Late one very hot afternoon, I decided to find a room for the night and get off the road early. I was in Tucumcari, New Mexico, and for some reason, all the hotels I checked were full with reservations. There must have been some big event taking place in the area.

Anyway, I finally checked one of the old run-down motels that had its heyday back before I-40 diverted nearly all traffic from Route 66 and changed the fortunes of the owners. Most of the doors to the rooms were open, and it was late in the day—after three o'clock. I just assumed their housekeeping staff had gotten a late start. I parked my bike in the shade of the only tree on the property and walked to the office. When I went in, there was no one there, and the sign still read, No Vacancy.

I started back toward the bike. As I was almost there, a woman came sprinting toward me from one of the open rooms and yelled, "If you wait a minute, I can make up a room for you. Meet me in the office."

I went in and paid for my room, and then offloaded most of my stuff from the bike. She must have been in a big hurry because the bed was just thrown together in no time at all. Anyway, the rate was super low, and I didn't care about the imperfect housekeeping. It was just a cheap place to crash for the night.

I headed out and found an out-of-the-way cantina where I drank some beers, shot some pool, and grabbed some dinner.

I headed back to my room early to get an early start the next day. When I turned down my sheets, I thought I noticed a couple of tiny red spots on the pillow case, almost like blood. I just turned the pillow over and went to sleep.

Three days later, while doing my laundry at Jacob Lake, Arizona, on my way up to the North Rim of the Grand Canyon, I noticed a terrible rash on my neck. I couldn't see it, but there was a string of hard itchy bumps, all in a row, on the back of my neck.

What could that be? I wondered.

I hadn't been walking through any tall grasses while pulled alongside any roads during piss stops, so I hadn't contacted anything like poison ivy. After thinking about it a while, I realized that the itching started after breaking into my second gear bag that held half of my clothes, none of which had been worn yet on that run until then. I called my wife Stacey and asked whether she had changed laundry detergent recently. She had. That must have been the source of the irritation. The shirt collar had been chafing my neck, and I probably had some allergic reaction to that new detergent. That was it, for sure, I told myself.

The next day while heading up to North Rim, I noticed a terrible itching on my right ankle. It was so annoying that I pulled over at one point and removed my boot and sock to have a look. There was a string of hard red bumps under my sock that felt the same as those on my neck.

That's just great! I thought. *Now I'm going to have to rewash all of my clothes to get that damned new detergent out of them.*

I pissed away several hours, first just waiting to use the machines at the North Rim camper store, and then washing *all* of the clothes I packed for the trip.

That should do it, I thought.

Before heading west toward So Cal—my ultimate destination—I made my way up to Sturgis from Grand Canyon for the rally. By the time I had made it to Sturgis, I was broken out in seven places with strings of these itchy bumps, despite having washed all of my clothes. The first strings had also grown in length, bump after itchy red bump!

Just to be sure I had gotten the offending detergent completely out of my clothes, I washed them all again at the on-site Laundromat at Kemp's Kamp, where I camped out during the rally.

I couldn't sleep in my tent the first night—the itching had become unbearable. So the next evening I rode back into Keystone and went into the pharmacy there to look for cortisone cream. They had none, but the woman working there asked me why I wanted it. I showed her the bumps on my neck.

She very discreetly whispered to me, "I'm a nurse, and I'm pretty sure you have scabies. You need to see a doctor."

I thought, *What the hell are* scabies?

Well, I found out. They are vicious parasites that bore in through your skin, leaving their eggs to hatch within their blood-rich host, thus the ever increasing strings of red itchy bumps. But where the hell did I get them?

The nurse suggested I ride into Rapid City and go to the emergency room where they would prescribe an ointment to treat them. So I saddled up and pulled into Rapid around 10:00 p.m. In the emergency room were plenty of other bikers, who had suffered mishaps during the rally—busted wrists, legs, and so on. I had to sit in the waiting room with them until the triage nurse called me in to see a doctor.

When I finally got called back, I was on fire, scratching everywhere. The late-seventy-something doctor was a real judgmental prick! He said to me as he looked down at me over the rim of his glasses, "Have you been with any unclean women lately?"

What the hell! That depended on what doc meant by "unclean," although I had a pretty good idea.

I answered truthfully, "No. Why?"

"You have scabies. They are transmitted person-to-person or from furniture—like a fabric couch—where an infected person has been."

Then it hit me: that bitch in Tucumcari never stripped the bed back at the motel—she only did a half-assed job of making the bed after whoever had slept in it the night before. The red spots I saw on the pillow were probably from someone whose scabies sores were bleeding. That thought creeped me out, I have to say. That would explain why washing my clothes—twice—had no effect. If anything, I had been contaminating my clean clothes keeping them all together!

The doctor gave me a prescription before discharging me. It was nearly midnight when I got out of the emergency room. Thank heaven the Walgreen's pharmacy is open late in Rapid City.

When the young clerk at the counter handed me a tube of cream, I read the instructions and ingredients. On reading "permethrin" on the label, I blurted out loud, "THAT'S A TERMITICIDE!"

I'll never forget what the clerk said without missing a beat and with a deadpan look on his face: "Bugs are bugs." I about pissed myself laughing!

Then, all I had to do was use that stuff after riding all the way back to Kemp's from Rapid. I reread the instructions, which said to cover the *entire body*, except the eyes, and to shower the next day. Thankfully, that year was the first time I brought a tent on the bike large enough to stand up in. In previous years, I had packed only a small one-person backpack tent.

I got in my tent and stripped naked after putting my gear bag with my clean clothes inside. Fortunately, I was limber enough to slather that cream all over my back by myself. I doubled up on every string of red bumps and combed that shit through my hair thoroughly. I didn't get much sleep that night because I had thrown my sleeping bag outside the tent, although I hadn't yet slept in it that trip because I had been in motels up until the rally. However, I had laid on it—although only briefly—after making camp. Still, why take a chance?

I slept on the bare nylon bottom of the tent. Fortunately, I was camped in a grassy site, which offered some cushioning over the hard ground. I just stared up at the nylon ceiling most of the night until the sky began to lighten the next morning.

I grabbed a towel and wrapped it around myself to walk down to the showers, carrying only my clothes bag. As I was showering, I suddenly realized that none of the red bumps itched anymore and most were already less intense. Then suddenly I busted out laughing, thinking about what the clerk had said: "Bugs are bugs." I guess if permethrin is good enough to kill termites, then it's good enough to kill scabies mites too and in only a single head-to-toe application!

I got dressed using the doubly washed clothes in the gear bag. I then went back to my site to get my sleeping bag and even my tent, holding on to each with a riding glove-covered hand—no way did I want any free-ranging scabies jumping back on me! I washed them both in hot water and baked them in a hot dryer.

I washed everything—again! That must have worked because for the remaining two weeks of my run, I didn't have any more outbreaks.

For the rest of that run, every time I thought about that bitch in Tucumcari, I would get pissed off. But every time I remembered "Bugs are bugs," I would laugh my ass off.

Everything balances out, I guess...

COPS DO HAVE A SENSE OF HUMOR

We motorcyclists who have spent decades on two wheels become indifferent to the unsafe, inconsiderate acts of other motorists in cages. It's better to simply take evasive action and avoid an accident than flip off an offending jerk while underway. That can escalate, and there's no such thing as a fender bender where car versus bike.

Despite this, I confess that I fell to the temptation of giving the finger to a guy who had cut me off some years ago while Stacey was on the back because his actions were blatantly unsafe and willful.

One August day, Stacey and I were leaving Ocean City, Maryland, headed west on US 50. While still in Ocean City, we were riding from one traffic light to the next behind a very slow driver, but I stayed put figuring that once we got past the last light before open road, he would pick up his pace.

A couple of minutes had passed after the last light and the speed limit changed from thirty-five to fifty-five miles per hour, yet that guy continued to putt along at about thirty. Everyone who had been stacking up on my rear fender was then stomping it to the floor and passing. But still that guy just putted along—that is, until I had a chance to pass.

As soon as I signaled and took to the left lane and rolled on the throttle, that guy floored it! I just kept on the throttle and caught up to the traffic that had left us behind moments earlier. The guy then tucked in behind me and stayed just yards off my rear fender.

We were approaching a tree-lined section of road, kind of like a tunnel of pines, where the Maryland state police often set up radar. Nevertheless, I whacked the throttle to get that guy off my ass, but right up through eighty miles an hour (in a 55), he stayed "parked" on my fender. I only wanted to get to where I could pull back into the right lane and let him pass, but the traffic coming out of the resorts was bumper-to-bumper even at highway speed that close to town. Only just a little farther ahead I saw that I could pull over with no one in the right lane, so I started to roll off the throttle—just as I passed the state trooper tucked in the trees running radar!

Well, the guy who had dropped back after I passed eighty miles an hour closed the gap between me and him, and by then, the trooper had his lights on and was in pursuit of him or me or us both.

I was finally able to move right, and then the guy behind me passed me and swerved into the right lane and jammed on his brakes right in front of me! I wanted to punch his throat in.

I jammed on my brakes, and then swerved to the right where there just happened to be the last thirty yards or so of merging lane from an on-ramp. As I did, I whacked the throttle and passed the guy on the right and pulled back in. As I passed, I flipped him the bird with my left hand.

Within seconds, the trooper pulled over the guy who had cut me off, and then proceeded to pull me over too.

Oh well, I had *been speeding,* I thought.

I was only trying to put distance between me and the jerk who was glued to my rear fender, so if the trooper understood why I was hauling ass, he might see fit to waive a speeding ticket…*maybe.*

The trooper got out of his car and rushed up to me, arms out-stretched, waving his hands while yelling, "Don't say a word. I saw the whole thing. Just wait here!"

And with that he turned and walked back to the driver in the car that had cut me off.

That was odd. What did he think I might try to say? Did he think I was going to try to explain my actions and possibly incriminate myself?

Twenty-five minutes passed, and we were baking in the August sun. Stacey was in a panic—she'd never been issued a ticket or even pulled over for anything (still holds to this day). I explained that no matter what, the worst that would happen alongside the road is

I would get one or more tickets and have to pay fines later, but we would be underway again before too long. The worst overall is the points and insurance bump that would go along with a few tickets, and those would sting for a few years. But I kept that to myself.

Finally, the trooper walked up to me with a grin on his face. Stacey was as perplexed as I but relieved.

He explained, "Everyone on the road saw the exchange between you and that guy, so I had to pull you both over."

He asked for my license and registration and told me to sit tight for a minute. I began to wonder for what exactly I had gotten pulled over. Speeding? Passing on the right merge lane? I figured he'd tell me soon enough after running my tags, along with how much I would have to pay the State of Maryland.

The trooper came back with an even broader smile on his face and explained, "Maryland has a new law such that whenever we pull someone over, we must at least write up a warning citation. We can't pull you over without a record of it explaining why you were stopped."

And with that, he handed me a warning citation slip but never said what it was for. Hell, I was relieved to know I was just getting a warning—no points and no fines was all I needed to learn and no need to say anything to my insurance company.

As I accepted the slip, the trooper went on to say—then through outright laughter—"Oh yeah, the last time I checked, this is the hand signal for a left turn [holding his left arm outstretched], and this is the signal for a right turn [holding his left arm out with his forearm up at a ninety-degree angle]."

Then he said, "Get on your bike and get out of here. I'll keep that guy here long enough for you to be miles down the road, and considering how much this stop is going to cost him, I don't think he'll be catching up to you."

"Thanks!"

I tossed the citation in the Tour Pak before Stacey and I got back on the bike quickly and rolled on down the highway.

Later that night while having dinner, my curiosity got the best of me. I went out to the bike and retrieved the ticket. By the light of our dinner table candle, I was able to read the citation, and then the whole exchange between me and the trooper became abundantly clear—and then I started to laugh out loud.

The trooper saw the other driver stuck on my rear fender, and then cut me off, and that I had to use evasive maneuvers to avoid running into his rear bumper, and that I "communicated" with the other driver as I passed him on the right with my outstretched left arm, including my solitary middle finger. That is, the trooper didn't see me as doing anything wrong under the circumstances, other than the warning scribbled on the citation: Improper use of hand signals.

I laughed as hard yesterday when I found that old citation as the day it happened, and I was grateful to have encountered a trooper with a sense of humor—and justice!

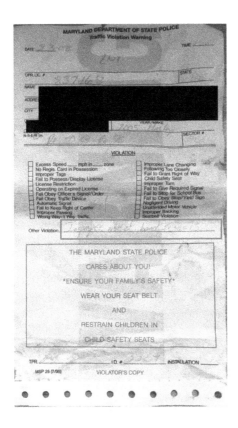

HONEST COP, DAMMIT!

Back during Sturgis '97, several of my friends were renting a house in Spearfish. One of them—Mike—had built an awesome pro-streeter based on the Sportster platform. He somehow ended up binding the rear brake caliper against the rotor, I think from too many burnouts and hole-shots. He likely snapped the rear wheel forward in the swing arm while dumping the clutch. In any case, the rear wheel was locked up tight. Mike needed a ride for himself and his bike. The rally wasn't even in full swing yet, and already we had a downed bike. Anyway, you stick by your friends and do what you can to keep them riding.

So Dennis and his girlfriend Laurie—some of Mike's Spearfish house crew—and I and Stacey raced back to Deadwood to borrow a tow vehicle and trailer from one of our friends who trailered his vintage Panhead to the rally.

While in Spearfish, Dennis and I were behind a guy from California, whose bike was the second vehicle stopped at a red light. Because he was turning right, he proceeded past the first car on the right, stopped, and then proceeded to make a right turn on red.

I pulled up and did the same thing. Dennis was about to follow but stopped short for some reason and waited for the light to change.

When the light changed, the cop who had pulled up behind Dennis shot around him and waved me over, and then proceeded past me and pulled over the guy from Cali too. What the hell!

It was a good fifteen minutes before the Cali rider pulled away and the cop came back to me. He ordered me into his vehicle and told Stacey to get up on the sidewalk.

For some bizarre reason, that deputy sheriff started to explain to me that the rider from Cali had no license on him, so he had to collect his fine on the spot. I certainly didn't need that information and didn't know what to think, but I asked him why he would let a rider go without a license.

The deputy explained that the guy had been pulled over previously for DUI and his license had been pulled on the spot. However, because such a suspect hasn't yet gone to trial, the court issues some kind of certificate, stating that the suspect has not been convicted—only charged—and thus still has driving privileges. However, there is no photo on this certificate, so anyone in possession close to meeting the description could use it. For that reason, the deputy either had to take the guy in, or if the guy consented, he could pay his fine on the spot and be on his way.

I was charged with the same bullshit offense: overtaking and passing in the same lane. Cost? Seventy-five bucks.

So I said to the deputy, "Well, I'm not gonna be here for a court date, so is there any way I can pay my fine now?"

"You want to pay me? Is that what you're saying?"

"Well, sure, if that's possible."

He handed me the written citation, and it showed the seventy-five-dollar fine. I reached in my vest pocket for my wallet and withdrew a one-hundred-dollar bill and handed it over. He put it on the seat and reached into his wallet and made change before telling me I was free to go. Before I concluded by business with the deputy, Dennis had snuck up alongside the passenger side of the vehicle and called out, "Jay!"

I turned my head instinctively in time for Dennis to snap my picture—so he could have lingering evidence of my detention—the prick!

After I stepped out from the car, I told Dennis what had transpired. He started laughing loudly.

"What's so funny, smart-ass?"

"You handed him a c-note, and he made change?"

"Yeah, why?"

Dennis went on, "This might be your lucky day."

"How do you figure? I'm out seventy-five bucks."

"You dumb son of a bitch! He pocketed that money. That stop doesn't exist—it'll never show up on your license. No points, no insurance bump."

"Get the hell outta here, Dennis. You've watched Serpico too many times!"

"Well, you'd better hope I'm right." He just laughed some more as he and Laurie headed back to his bike.

We pressed on and got our friend's F-150 and trailer. I left my bike and drove the truck with Stacey. I agreed to follow Dennis and Laurie to where Mike was stranded somewhere alongside the road.

Route US 85 that climbs up out of Deadwood is normally posted sixty-five miles per hour, but during the rally, it had been knocked down to fifty-five.

Well, Dennis got a wild hair up his ass and ripped up that hill. No way could I keep up with them in the truck. I rolled up to sixty-five miles an hour, and as I was rounding the first long turn, a police car was heading toward us from the other direction. As soon as we were in full view, its lights came on.

Shit, Dennis, thanks a lot! I thought.

I pulled over and waited for the cruiser to make a U-turn and tuck in behind us. While the trooper walked up to my window, I noticed his partner walking up real low on the passenger side—really? For a speeding stop!

Anyway, I lowered my window and shut off the engine. The trooper was apologetic—he repeatedly said that there's a zero tolerance order during the rally. Otherwise, he would've just gotten me to slow down. What really sucked was that sixty-five miles per hour is the normal speed on that road! Oh well…

I also told that trooper that I wasn't going to appear for a court date and asked whether I could pay on the spot. He said, "Wait here," before walking back to his cruiser.

When he returned, he had my citation, an admission-of-guilt form, and an envelope in his hands.

I tried to hand him exact change for the speeding fine, but unlike the deputy sheriff in Spearfish, that trooper wouldn't touch the money.

Hmm…maybe Dennis *was* right.

The trooper said, "I can't take that. I need you to read and sign this first [admission of guilt] and put that in the envelope."

I did as he asked and turned it over to him, but he balked again.

"I can't take that. I need you to put your fine in the envelope and seal it."

Holy shit! Dennis *must* have been right. That trooper was following some protocol to the letter.

I then tried to hand over the sealed envelope containing my citation, my admission of guilt, and my cash, but he still wouldn't touch it.

"Sir, now I need you to sign your name over the seal."

Yeah, at that point, there was no doubt that Dennis was right. That deputy made an easy hundred and fifty bucks—half from me, the other half from that guy from Cali!

After I signed the back of the envelope, only then did the trooper take possession and again apologize for no tolerance during the rally.

We pulled away, not sure exactly where we were headed to rescue Mike. Not far up the road, however, Dennis had pulled over, waiting for us. He and Laurie mounted up and accelerated quickly and resumed the lead. We got Mike and his down bike and got him safely back to the house in Spearfish, where he fixed his brakes.

Later during rally week, Dennis and Laurie and Stacey and I were heading back to Deadwood. About a mile from the steep drop-off along US 85 into the main road into Deadwood from Sturgis, traffic came to a crawl—the rally was then in full swing.

As we paddle-walked our bikes toward that final hill, I happened to look up and saw an amazing Victorian house way up on the hill overlooking the town below. The place was magnificent and huge and, no doubt, a high-dollar piece of real estate.

I pointed this out to Dennis and Laurie.

Dennis said authoritatively, "I know who lives up there!"

I was stunned that Dennis knew anyone in South Dakota.

I asked, "Who?"

Dennis shot back. "The sheriff!" before busting out laughing.

"Screw you, Dennis!"

But I have to admit, that was funny as hell! I guess my seventy-five-dollar fine had to go somewhere.

Two months after the rally, my bike insurance was due. Sure enough, Dennis was right. That deputy sheriff buried that "passing" citation, while the trooper—honest bastard—turned in my fine and the record for speeding. I paid a 20 percent insurance surcharge for three years thanks to that reported ticket. If only the trooper had been dishonest too, it would have *saved* me money.

Never thought I would prefer a corrupt cop over a straight arrow, but I was leaning that way after getting my insurance statement!

LEARNING ABOUT SPARK ADVANCE, THE HARD WAY (PART 1)

In order for an engine to develop optimal power from the fuel-air charge in the cylinder, it must actually be ignited *before* the piston reaches the top of the cylinder, or top dead center (TDC), so that it is completely burned at a certain point after TDC to get the most power. In a car, idle spark timing might be something like eight degrees BTDC (before TDC). Various mechanical and, eventually, electronic means have been employed to not only advance spark timing after starting an engine but also to continuously advance it as much as sixty degrees BTDC as the engine revolutions per minute (rpm) increases so that the mixture is always completely burned at the same point of the piston downstroke.

An engine's spark timing must start out at zero degrees, or TDC (or even be slightly retarded), so that while the engine is cranking at very low rpm, it cannot kick back and rotate in the wrong direction when the fuel-air charge is ignited on the piston upstroke. Once an engine is spinning fast enough, the spark can be advanced because momentum prevents any kickback, and as mentioned already, spark advance is required for optimal burn and power.

My first bike, a 1977 FXE, had a kick starter, and unbeknownst to me back then, the spark was advanced automatically only when the rpm was greater than about three hundred—far faster than any human could kick it. That is, there was no advance until after the bike was running and thus no chance for kick back while starting. Advance occurred after starting by centrifugal force from tiny weights on the points plate in the cone bottom of a Shovelhead Harley motor—quite simple, really.

What I didn't know, as a cocky nineteen-year-old who had been kick-starting the FXE for a couple of years, is that before the '69 Shovelhead, the rider had to manually advance the timing after starting the bike, which *also* meant he had to *retard* the spark before kicking it to life, else risk kickback.

Spark timing on a Panhead, Knucklehead, or Flathead was accomplished manually through the left grip on the handlebar. Just as you twisted the right throttle grip toward you to go faster, you twisted the left grip toward you to advance the spark and, conversely, away from you to retard it. Harley spark timing in those older engines was very crude—it was "off/on." Either it was retarded fully for starting or advanced twenty-five degrees, whether idling or wide open throttle. The twenty-five-degree maximum was controlled by a slot that limited the travel of the spark timer, which was mounted in the engine case.

(Note: Many who are unaware of "waste spark ignition" incorrectly identify a Harley spark timer as a "distributor." A distributor has a rotor to send spark to a specific spark plug wire, one at a time. Carbureted Harleys fired both plugs all the time. It's just that one would be on the exhaust stroke and did nothing [the "wasted" spark], while the other was on its power stroke.)

Starting the FXE cold required rolling on the throttle twice to squirt raw gas into the intake tract—with or without the choke—and then turning on the ignition before kicking the bike to life. Because the simple Linkert carburetor on my friend's '51 Panhead had no accelerator pump, unlike the FXE, you had to set the choke full, kick twice to draw raw fuel into the intake, then set the choke to half before turning on the ignition prior to kicking. Other than that slight change in the order of steps, what else could there have been to starting an older bike?

Well, I'm here to tell you that stiff-legging the starter shaft while the spark is advanced from the last person who rode the bike will launch a 150-pound nineteen-year-old clear over the bike and elicit unending laughter from the older experienced bikers who were standing by, anticipating the results of old iron ignorance!

I was pissed off! No way was I going to give up. On my second attempt, I didn't stiff-leg the kicker, which only proved worse. My foot slipped off the kicker pedal just as the fuel-air charge ignited on the upstroke, sending the kicker in reverse, stopping only when it contacted my calf. The black-and-blue knot that was left on my leg served as a permanent reminder (once they showed me how to retard the spark) to always roll off on the left grip before kicking any old iron to life, even to this day.

They got me! The old guys had a good laugh at my expense. But I never again forgot to check spark timing on an old bike, I can tell you that. It also taught me that a bunch of old grizzled bikers aren't the most compassionate bunch while you're hobbling around with a huge purple knot on your kicker leg!

Learning about Spark Advance, the Hard Way (Part 2)

The oldest Harley I have ever ridden was a 1930 VL. It wasn't my bike, and I blew up the motor in it.

Without going into the thermodynamic details, when the spark timing for an engine is not advanced enough the engine will run hotter than it would with proper spark advance.

Setting the spark timing in an old Harley is quite simple. You remove the timing plug from the left side of the engine case, exposing the massive flywheel. Roll off the left grip for no spark advance. Next, loosen the lock screw that holds the stout steel wire that is connected to the spark timer and controlled by the left handlebar grip so the spark timer can rotate to the "zero" end of its slot. Next, use the kick start pedal to rotate the engine until the timing mark appears in the hole. Adjust your points until they open just as the timing mark is centered in the hole. That sets zero degrees of spark advance. Replace the timing plug when done. Then, when you rotate the left grip all the way after starting, the engine advances twenty-five degrees.

That is what I had done to tune up my friend's VL. That is *exactly* what I had done, unfortunately. I missed the crucial step of retightening the hold down screw on the spark advance wire.

After tuning, I went for the usual test ride. The bike fired easily with the new points installed and settled into the expected idle after I advanced the spark.

After riding for maybe ten miles, the bike just seemed to be running flat; it was losing power. It was a cold November day, and I didn't feel like troubleshooting along the road. So I just flogged the throttle to get back quickly. The longer I rode, the less power it had, so I gave it even more throttle. That proved to be exactly the wrong thing to do.

The bike lost more power until finally I heard a bad noise from the engine and lost most of my speed while bluish white smoke poured from the exhaust—the motor had blown.

I flagged down a motorist and asked for a ride to the nearest pay phone. I had a friend pick up me and the dead bike. On tearing down the motor, I discovered a hole the size of a nickel in the rear piston! What the hell!

The hole explained the power loss and smoking, but what could explain the hole?

It wasn't long before I discovered the missing lock down screw for the spark timer wire. The wire comes in at a hard angle and so didn't slip initially. But the vibration after ten miles of running allowed the spark timer to retard the spark to at least zero degrees. That severely overheated the engine, melting a hole in the aluminum piston.

I nearly ended a good friendship over that stupid mistake, but luckily, a friend who went to every motorcycle swap meet in our area actually had a new-old-stock VL piston *in the original box*. It cost me $35 back in 1981, but it saved a friendship. And besides, it was my fault.

Ever after that stupid mistake, I have double-checked every step of every procedure while wrenching on my Harleys, and cars too. Some lessons are learned the hard way but then are never forgotten!

RON'S RADIO DEBUT

After work one Friday night back in '92, my friend Ron and I decided to ride our Harleys three hundred miles north to his family's hunting camp in Bradford County, Pennsylvania, to do some early-season trout fishing in the secluded no-name wild native brook trout streams within miles of their camp.

Ron was a member of the primary response team (PRT) at the DuPont Experimental Station where we both worked at the time. He decided it would be a good idea to borrow a pair of PRT radios for us to use in the woods so we could split up and cover more water. These were voice-activated and allowed us to stay in touch so that if one or the other of us were consistently hooking up, we could call the other to join in on more productive water.

We strapped all our gear—fishing tackle, clothes, rainsuits, and warm layers—to Ron's '89 FXSTC Softail Custom and my '92 FXSTS Softail Springer and headed out right after work.

The Friday night traffic on that, the first nice weekend in May, was brutal until we got north of Harrisburg.

We ate at some remote truck stop, and when we resumed our run, it was well after dark. Night riding never bothered me, but more deer are killed on Pennsylvania highways each year than are harvested by archery, muzzleloader, shotgun, and rifle hunters combined. Consequently, we rode slowly on all the secondary roads all the way to Ron's camp nearly to the New York border.

Despite passing many browsing deer, none crossed our paths. However, a fox gave Ron a sphincter-pucker moment. He crushed his front fork and locked his back wheel avoiding a collision as the fox shot across the road in front of him. It was close!

When we got to camp, we had to turn on the water, gas, and electric before settling in around 2:00 a.m. Despite our late arrival, we arose around 6:00 a.m. to head to town for groceries, which we brought back to cook at the cabin. We got eggs and bacon, toast and coffee—just the right fare to prime us for all-day fishing.

Ron was the most hardcore fisherman I had ever met. He would hit the water at dawn and fish until dusk and no matter how the weather would change during the day and whether or not he had any rain gear or warmer layers on hand. So I knew that breakfast was the only thing I would get to eat until we cooked dinner on returning to the cabin after dark. As such, I ate six eggs and half of the pound of bacon Ron cooked in the huge iron skillet, in which just about every meal in camp was cooked.

We rode only about five miles from the cabin before Ron pulled over just before a tiny stone bridge. The "stream" was little more than a ditch. I was pissed off. I thought to myself, *I rode three hundred miles for this!*

Neither of our bikes had locking saddlebags, and so we stowed the bikes in the woods as far off the road as we dare ride with highway tires.

As it turned out, that "ditch" gradually widened to, at most, twelve feet wide. There was nowhere along its course more than a foot deep. Little did I know on arriving that I was about to get the most important stream fishing lessons of my life—lessons that I have put to use countless times over to put fish in the net since Ron schooled me that weekend.

Ron patiently explained what he knew about stream fishing for trout. I paid attention and just did as he instructed. We caught more than fifty wild native brookies from that "ditch" that day before heading back to camp for a fresh trout dinner. Ron also showed me a superior technique for filleting small stream-run trout that I still use today.

I learned to read trout water that day, and the rigging choices that Ron shared with me have produced consistently ever since. I learned too that tiny streams can hold an incredible number of fish—behind almost every rock or fallen tree.

We gorged ourselves on fresh fish back at camp. Because there was no TV or radio back at the cabin, we turned in early. We would need the rest—Ron had planned for us to fish a large river the next day.

Breakfast on day 2 consisted of eggs and fish sandwiches. Because we had to head back that day, we closed up the cabin and planned to fish for only a half day. Knowing Ron, he would want to cover as much water as possible in the time we had.

I don't remember the name of the river he took me to, but we fished upstream from the paper mill in the tiny town we rode through to get to it. Thankfully, the wind was in our favor because on passing the mill, we both were gagging on the unmistakable odor of pyridine coming from the stacks.

Ron and I had very different fishing styles on big water, but each worked equally well. Ron preferred to make a few casts and move on through quickly. I preferred to make several casts, and then change up rigs or flies and thoroughly work a piece of water before moving on. Plus, Ron always tried to work a piece of water ahead of me—a trait that landed him in the water many times after trying to wade too quickly across slimy rocks in the Salmon River while trying to cover the best pools ahead of me.

Because we didn't stick together like the day before, we used the voice-activated PRT radios to keep tabs on each other. At first, we chatted every few minutes or so about the fishing conditions we each were experiencing. But the sessions became fewer and further spaced. In fact, I eventually forgot I even had the radio with me, much less turned on, until out of the blue, I heard the most godawful commotion come over the radio, which was punctuated by the sound of brush and breaking branches, before ending in a huge splashing sound accompanied with lots of swearing.

I knew what happened; I was dying laughing!

I spoke into the radio and said, through tears of laughter, "You fell in, didn't you!"

All I heard was, "FUCK YOU!" followed by the clicking sound as Ron turned off his radio.

I almost fell off the bank myself at that point. I was doubled over laughing, just picturing the scene that I had just heard but did not see, although the mental picture was priceless!

I gathered up my gear and headed upstream toward Ron's general direction, still laughing. I saw Ron emerge from the stream bank. He was covered in mud and soaking wet from asshole to shoe sole! I started laughing again—I couldn't help it.

Ron had regained his composure by the time I caught up with him such that he was laughing then too.

We walked back to our bikes, secured our gear, and headed home from a great weekend of fishing, combined with a long relaxing Harley ride.

Ron was killed in 1995 in a snowmobile accident while running poachers off his family's hunting camp in New York. I've never forgotten what he taught me about stream trout fishing—or his water landing broadcast over the radio that day!

Thanks for the laughs, friend.

CRAAAAZY YANKEES!

Years ago, when I worked in Delaware, my good friend Gabby and I would hit the road on our bikes every weekend chance we got. More often than not, we would run down to Seneca Rocks, West Virginia, and stay at the motel at the crossroads right across from the Rocks. During warmer months, however, we couldn't always get a room there because it is a popular rock climbing destination. Still, without any concrete plans for a room for the night, we would head down anyway and chance getting a room over the mountain in Franklin or back in Petersburg.

Gabby was the person who got me watching *South Park* mostly because he would quote the Eric Cartman character, and I had no idea what he was talking about until I tuned in. Through Gabby, I learned that fat-ass Cartman liked sweets and treats, like "pah," his corrupted way of saying "pie."

Some of our West Virginia weekend road trips were nothing less than surreal for the bizarre shit that happened along the way, like this one time we stayed at Yokum's.

We tried to get a room at Seneca Rocks one warm May weekend but got shut out by others with reservations. We had taken the day off work that Friday and needed a room for two nights, whether at one place or different ones on Friday and Saturday.

We doubled back up the road a piece to Yokum's, which is only maybe five miles back from the Rocks. Yokum's consists of a small motel just off the road with a small restaurant and some rental cabins out back. We decided to grab a bite to eat.

While talking to the young waitress, we asked if they had any rooms left for the night. They did, and so we paid for the room before grabbing dinner. The young girl painstakingly did the math to add tax to the quoted room rate. Gabby and I both suppressed our laughter while she managed to do her "ciphering" before handing us the room receipt and key. She then led us into the restaurant from the motel check-in area.

They served us some great Southern cooking, and each time the young waitress left our table, Gabby would start mimicking her heavy Southern accent and a cross between that and Eric Cartman. I was choking on my dinner trying not to laugh!

While eating, we decided that rather than take a chance on finding a room the next night, we might just as well stay put at Yokum's.

So I took our room receipt back to the motel check-in area and asked our waitress whether it was also available the following night. It was, so I took out exact change to pay for the second night. But the waitress was totally befuddled and had to go into the back room and ask for help to figure out how much money it would cost, plus tax, for two nights at the same rate—duh, twice the amount for the first night! She resorted to using a calculator to do the math all over again, and you know what? It came to exactly what I had in my hand!

Oh my god! That poor sweet girl was thick. And of course, Gabby heard the whole exchange and was laughing himself silly back at our table, loud enough that I could hear him. And—no doubt—so could our clueless waitress, who just kept a perfect smile on her face the whole time!

I was almost in tears when I got back to the table, and every time my laughter would finally subside, Gabby would start back in quoting our math-challenged waitress in Eric Cartman's voice. My stomach muscles hurt from laughing so hard!

When the noise from our table subsided, our waitress came back with that clueless innocent smile on her face and as pleasant as could be to ask, "Would y'all like some dessert?"

I asked, "What do you have?"

"We have different kinds o' pah."

Gabby lost it and literally spit out most of the last bite of his dinner all over the table. Our waitress didn't even respond—she just kept beaming away, waiting for us to answer her.

I managed to blurt out, "No, just the check, please…"

Our waitress headed back into the kitchen from where we heard her say to the woman who schooled her in basic math, "Them Yankees is craaaazy!"

On hearing that, Gabby and I laughed even harder still! At every other place we stopped to eat that trip, Gabby would ask me, "Y'all gonna have some PAH with that?" and I would crack up all over again.

Maybe we were just craaaazy Yankees!

A WEEKEND PUTT

I had to take off one Friday in July 2015 to take care of some home-owner insurance issues. That only took until noon, so what else was a fellow to do with the wife out of town and no weekend agenda? I tell you what: time for a road trip!

I generally don't make any concrete plans when I go on the road. That's part of the fun of seeing America from the saddle of a Harley—you just go wherever you get the urge to at the moment.

After a tasty buffalo burger at the Proud Cut Saloon, I saddled up and headed east with general plans to hit the Black Hills over in South Dakota. I decided two things on leaving: keep off the Super Slab (I-90) as much as possible and hold down my speed to reasonable levels. I kept true on the first point, not so much on the second.

Within minutes of leaving Cody on US 16, it started to rain gently. I could see the cloud line, so I just ducked behind the fairing on the '14 Electra Glide Ultra and rode it out.

By the time I made it to Eagle Ridge, the rain was done for the rest of the trip—while I was in the saddle, at least. I took US 16 over the Bighorns and then on to I-90 past Gillette. Route 16 and I-90 are one in the same road for that stretch, and when you get off for Moorcroft, you are back on old US 16 as a separate road again.

I got a room in Moorcroft Friday night and went to the grocery store to buy supplies for an in-room dinner. Shortly after getting settled in, a hellacious thunderstorm blew through. It was the kind you know won't last and the kind you enjoy for the light show. I sat under the overhang outside of my room and ate a light dinner of fresh vegetables, cheese, and beer while watching the lightning and all the while smiling to myself because I had ridden one more day without having to don rain gear.

When the storm broke, you could see the red sunset below the black cloud deck, and all you could smell was the scent of wet sagebrush, blowing in on the breeze. Any day on the road when you make it to your resting spot for the night before the heavens open up is a good one. The bike was filthy from the ride over, but after the rainstorm, only a little bug residue was left behind. And all the dust and pollen were gone.

I awoke the next morning at 5:30 a.m. to dead calm air and cloudless blue sky at fifty degrees. It was time for the leathers—but not before breakfast.

I don't usually eat breakfast most days, but when I'm on the road or camping, it is a ritual. Fresh coffee, eggs, home-fries, bacon, and toast—all the things I avoid usually—are routine on the road. The motel I stayed at was right next door to the only café in Moorcroft, so I didn't have far to go to "fuel up." The temp had risen to fifty-eight by the time I saddled up, so I put on the chaps and a sweatshirt jacket under my vest and rolled on without the leather jacket. I knew from many years of riding it would be chilly for the first hour or so but quickly heat up in the high plains now that the sun was up and unimpeded by a single cloud.

I rolled on over to the Hills on US 16 through New Castle, the self-proclaimed "Sagebrush Capital of the World." Border towns like New Castle, Beulah, and Hulett are unique and atypical of other eastern Wyoming towns because they are either in or very close to Wyoming's Black Hills, which gives them a semi-mountain appeal, unlike a town like Kaycee, which is hot, desolate, and boring as hell.

I really like riding through the Black Hills of South Dakota. The roads are a nice balance of rolling straightaways and twisty curves. I remember thinking that I would much rather be there then than in three weeks during the Sturgis Rally when the roads would be jammed with inexperienced riders who only know how to flog the throttle in the straightaways but go pitifully slow through the curves because they don't know how to lean and "see a line" through turns. But my ride was not to be free and easy after all.

I saw a sign hanging from one of the casinos in Deadwood that read: Welcome, Rally-goers.

Kind of early, I thought.

As it turned out, there was a Corvette rally in full swing. And I'm here to tell you, it might as well have been a *Chevette* rally for as slow and pokey as those drivers were! Sure, they would roll on to about seventy miles an hour in the straights, but on the turns—which *any* recent 'vette can carve even faster than my bike—they would slow down worse than the worst newbie Harley rider. I couldn't believe it.

Now, don't get me wrong—I don't mind rolling through the Hills at a slow pace but at least a *consistent* one. Rolling on the throttle and going through fourth, fifth, and sixth gear continuously gets real old real quick on a bike while stuck behind a line of 'vettes as far as one could see through the next turn. So I did the only logical thing—I whacked the throttle up to 110 and passed them all! Once I had little 'vettes in my rearview, the ride became free and easy in the Hills thereafter. So much for sticking to my second decision point at the outset of the ride!

I stopped at Trevino's Leathers, which is a must-see for any biker looking for some chaps, a vest, or even full-on leather coveralls for winter riding. On the steps leading up to the log-cabin-like shop, there were baskets full of rabbit skins. I knew immediately I would have to buy *something* on realizing Trevino had a sick twisted sense of humor like mine: the sign in one of the baskets read "Empty Bunnies" and the price.

Turns out I made a purchase after all and regardless of the empty bunny humor. I got Stacey a purple motorcycle-chain-like bracelet with Swarovski crystals between the links. Purple is her favorite color, and so I was hoping it would be a welcomed surprise on seeing her at the airport when she returned on Sunday.

Because I had gotten such an early start on Saturday, I got a wild hair up my ass to ride over to Wall through the Badlands. But first, I had to make a stop in Keystone to check out the Holy Terror Mine antique shop. That shop always has interesting Disney memorabilia from as far back as the 1930s. Stacey is a die-hard Disney fan and collector. So when I spot stuff she might like, I send her a text with pictures. That time, I got off easy—she already had one of everything the store had on hand that day.

Instead of fighting Rapid City traffic, I took South Dakota 40 (SD 40) from Keystone over to SD 79 on down to SD 44. Two-lane SD 44 runs the width of the state, running approximately parallel to I-90 and between twenty and forty miles south of the interstate—my kind of road. It runs right on through Badlands National Park. One spur drops down into Wall, which I took because I had ridden through the Badlands on many other trips and the temperature was already in the mid-eighties by then. It was time for my free glass of ice water at Wall Drug, which was once a draw for motorists to stop in Wall during the thirties and forties. Being on the bike, however, I opted to buy a bottle of water instead and head back on the road.

You can't see America from the interstate, so unless making time is a factor, I'll take the roads less traveled every time while in the saddle. I jumped back on I-90 west until I could exit the Super Slab and head to SD 34. South Dakota route 34 is a mirror of SD 44—it runs the width of the state and is roughly parallel to I-90 and between twenty and forty miles north of it. Plus, SD 34 drops right into Sturgis from the north after passing Bear Butte. I figured as long as I was that close to "biker mecca," I might as well drop on in.

Coming from the north, you eventually see a giant steel silhouette of a buffalo with cut out letters that read PIHC, backward for C-H-I-P, when viewed from the north. Coming *from* Sturgis, however, one immediately recognizes that as the Buffalo Chip campground where the best Rally concerts are held. Both big-name rock 'n' roll and country performers entertain at the Chip while all manner of biker shenanigans are taking place under their noses. It's a partying place for sure. Well, it would be in another three weeks—that is, during the seventy-fifth annual Black Hills Motor Classic, or just "Sturgis" rally for most bikers.

On the way into town from the north, you pass by City Park. I first attended the rally in 1981, the year the city fathers nearly voted against ever having another rally in Sturgis, and for good reason too. What might be hard for a modern-era biker to comprehend is that in '81, the *entire rally* was in City Park, and nearly everyone camped out. There were probably only 4,500 people there. When I returned in 1995 for the fifty-fifth, I was in utter shock. By '95, the rally drew *several hundred thousand* riders from all over the world. And *most* stayed in motels, rented houses, or in their motor homes, and most trailered their bikes there! The rally had become commercial gold. At 10:00 p.m., you are likely today to see tourists gawking at the riders on the street while pushing their baby carriage! Not so in 1981.

In '81, only the hardcore attended. Riders rode to the rally— no "trailer queen" bikes. Sure, someone's old lady might have driven a chase vehicle, but that was needed to throw a broken-down Shovelhead in the back to take back to camp to wrench on it for the next day's riding. I don't miss my Shovelhead—wrench on Saturday so you could ride on Sunday…maybe. The Evolution engine that saved the Motor Company was two years from existence at that point.

Anyway, during the '81 rally, the one-percenters were there in full force. Many of them were strapped with side-arms, which many of the Hells Angels were, anticipating trouble from another club. No gunfights materialized, but a few people I saw got cut badly. But that wasn't what irked the town fathers.

Sturgis '81 for a twenty-year-old kid was awesome! The rival clubs would do stuff like blow up other clubs' port-o-potties with sticks of dynamite, and the shit—literally—would fly everywhere. Then, some drunks harassed and threatened some city workers who were there to drop off free firewood, and it went downhill from there. The state militia was called, and it was anybody's guess what might happen if you tried to get some sleep. It was a twenty-four-hour party. The mess the clubs made was disgraceful, and the City of Sturgis didn't want another rally *ever*. But the cooler heads prevailed, and the rally continued to become the phenomenon it is today. Nowadays, I have been told, the Red and White *own* several hotels and downtown rally-only shops. That's progress for you!

On finally arriving Saturday on Main Street—the heart of the rally—I was amazed. Most of the vendors were already set up, and the rally doesn't officially start until August 1. That was good for me though because I hate the size of the crowds that rally week brings. I found what I had come for and got out.

For every year I attended the rally, I've gotten the official Sturgis Rally enameled pins. That year—the seventy-fifth—would be no different. Every vendor had them. So I got my rally pins and some souvenirs and beat feet back to my bike to get out of town.

I decided to stay the night in Aladdin, Wyoming—population fifteen. The only businesses in Aladdin are the one hundred-plus-year-old store and the café-motel right next door. Back in 2000 or so, the motel was a rat's nest. Since then, however, a new ten- or twelve-room motel has been built, which is quite nice and reasonable too—less than $65 for my room—and they let me park the bike outside my door under the breezeway. I called ahead for a room because even though I was close, there is nowhere to eat in Aladdin late in the day, so I knew it would take me a while to eat in Belle Fourche before making the last eighteen miles or so to Aladdin.

After a great walleye dinner, I rolled on over to Aladdin to end another perfect day in the saddle. I wasn't tired at 8:00 p.m., so I walked the road for about three miles before returning to my room. It's amazing how many whitetails I scared up while walking the road, but not while rolling past at sixty-five miles an hour on a Milwaukee Vibrator. I'm glad they stayed put—there's no such thing as a fender bender between a bike and a deer!

I had planned to rise again at first light but really didn't *need* to get on the road that early to do my thing and make it back to Cody in time for Stacey's 9:00 p.m. flight. Plus, if I delayed the start of the ride back, I wouldn't need to leather up at all—it would be plenty warm by 10:00 a.m., checkout time.

I rolled on nice and easy over to Hulett before heading up to Devils Tower. I had been to the tower a dozen times or more over the years, but I headed there for breakfast in the little café in the gift shop just outside of the National Monument entrance gate. Across the road from the café-shop is a KOA campground with its own gift shop now, which I had never been in. I decided to check it out.

There was nothing of interest inside the shop for me. However, they sell "Cactus" brand ladies' shirts, which Stacey loves for the fit and style and because they are USA-made. I found one with a biker-themed Route 66 print, which I bought on the spot. Only problem was, I couldn't be sure of her size, and I damn sure wasn't about to go on the *high* side of getting the wrong size. Women are funny about shit like that! So while I might have unblinded my hand, I texted Stacey to verify her size, and it was a good thing too. I put my pick back on the rack for the next *smaller* size. Whew—dodged that bullet!

After leaving the tower, I decided to return to Moorcroft to follow old US 16 into Gillette to stop at the Harley dealer. Despite the spot-on GPS directions to get me there, the Harley dealer in Gillette is closed on Sunday. Oh well, who really cares when you have no purposeful destination on a road trip? Certainly not me.

I pressed on to US 14, north of Gillette, to ride the old road over to Sheridan. And while that was a last-minute course correction, I deviated farther still. Outside of Gillette, I saw the sign for Broadus, Montana, along WY 59—why not?

On a very unusually warm weekend back in March, I found myself up in Broadus, where I was held up in their café as a tornado touched down momentarily across the road. My '98 Electra Glide was nearly blown over against the weight on the kickstand. I have no idea what the f-rating of that brief twister was or even if it made the news, but I was damn glad I turned back into town when the storms blew up because I would have had no shelter along that stretch of US 212.

But that Sunday was a blue-sky day and pleasant riding, except for the sideways strong straight-line winds that were blowing me and a nearly nine hundred-pound bike from the centerline to the fog line on a shoulder-less two-lane. I headed to Broadus to have a late-day lunch, but the café there was also closed on Sunday.

I decided to continue on US 212 west all the way until it joins back up with I-90, about a hundred miles away. Where it does rejoin the interstate is close to the site of Custer's Last Stand. I thought I would eat at the Native American-owned café there—maybe a nice Indian fry-bread taco salad. However, the headwind just wouldn't quit, and I lost about ten miles per gallon fighting it all along 212. So when I noticed a small sign to turn south toward Sheridan and Kirby, I made the turn.

I knew about the Kirby Saloon, so if I couldn't hold out for dinner until Sheridan or Dayton, I could stop there. The Kirby Saloon sits by itself with nothing else around it in a nice green treed valley. After only about ten miles of riding that road south, the winds that had pushed me around most of the afternoon were quelled by the high ground and trees along that route. I could then roll on hard through the twisties again, without concern for getting blown over enough to drag metal on asphalt.

Unfortunately, while that road is protected from the wind, there were bad buckles or seams regularly spaced in the asphalt, which were pile-driving my wrists on every bump. That prevented leaning over far in turns too to prevent loss of control on the worst of the bumps. Eventually, that road drops back down into Wyoming, where you pick up WY 338 to get back over to I-90, six miles west of Sheridan and six miles east of the Ranchester-Dayton exit and US 14. I jumped on I-90 at the port of entry and immediately took the Acme exit, which puts you on old 14, the "Black Diamond Trail," which is named for the once-prolific coal mining in the area and which runs right into Ranchester. From there, it is only about 130–140 miles back to Cody.

Being it was Sunday, traffic would be light going up the mountain but heavy coming down as all the weekenders would be pulling their RVs back to civilization.

I decided to eat dinner at the café in Dayton for two reasons: to get the timing right for the weekend traffic and to avoid the ugly black thunderhead that was forming over the Bighorns.

After my slab pork-chop dinner, I was ready for a nap! I couldn't linger then though because it was getting late enough that I had to make time to meet Stacey back in Cody at the airport. Making time over the mountain was never a concern for me because pushing the Harley hard over through the turns and maintaining full speed ahead was kind of the whole point in two-wheeled transportation for me. If you don't scrape the back corners off the running boards, you aren't pushing hard enough through the twisties. I had gone through four sets of running boards on my '98!

It was eighty-six degrees when I left Dayton, but by the time I was on top of the Bighorns where the storm had just passed through, it was fifty-six. Nevertheless, I didn't stop to leather up. I knew on the Basin side it would be warm again, so I just rode out the chill and basked in the warm air of Shell Canyon on the downside.

I made it to the airport at 8:40 p.m.—eighteen minutes before Stacey's flight was scheduled to touch down.

Stacey had been out of town for the entire week, first on business, and then to visit with friends. She always likes it when I greet her at the airport on her return home. Truth is, I like to see her on her return too.

On seeing me in the terminal in my riding vest, she asked, "Oh, have you been riding?"

"Oh, just a little weekend putt," I replied.

The odometer told a different story when I finally parked in the garage at home. In two and a half days, I had clocked 1,284 miles… just because.

BAD PUPPY KARMA

My friend Paul had dropped his 2017 FLHTCU several times over a year's span or so. He complained that the new bikes are much taller and heavier than his 2000 FLHTCU or his 1977 FLH had been. He was right—my 2019 FLHTCU tips the scales wet at 906 pounds! That's about 350 pounds more that most of the Harley cruisers I had owned over the years, and the saddle height was about three inches taller too. So I think all that talk about higher centers of gravity, taller saddle height, increased weight, and so on must have jinxed me or something. More on that later.

I was watching the sun set from my campsite in Beulah, Wyoming, one night back in July (2020), ready to turn in for an early start the following day, when Curly, the campground host, rolled up in his golf cart and invited me to go up the road to Saloon 333 for a nightcap. Seeing as how it was only about 8:30 p.m., I accepted. I grabbed my Streamlight flashlight from the tent so I could see in my Tour Pak to secure my sidearm, after which we rode up to the bar.

The bartender was a take-no-shit Blackfoot-Cherokee twenty-four-year-old maiden who knew Curly and gave him shit the whole time we were there. I enjoyed that immensely, considering Curly is a retired construction business owner and veteran Seabee. He didn't know what to say, especially when the bartender tried to guilt him with a tale of her people being killed off by "his people" from smallpox-infected blankets given to her tribe by the US government! Before she laid in on Curly with that White guilt trip, she winked at me to let me know something was coming. I about pissed myself laughing! Curly, who had been very vocal up to that point, was speechless—until Miss Native American started laughing at him hysterically. Only then did he realize he'd been had!

When another patron, who had ridden to the bar on a four-wheeler, was ready to leave, Curly grabbed me and said we needed to follow him because his golf cart had no headlights.

I went to pay for my drinks, but the bartender said Curly already had. I wasn't expecting a free ride, but I made sure to thank him back in the golf cart.

Following the lighted four-wheeler was easy enough along the road, but the driver had to continue past the campground turn off. Once we were riding blind, Curly quickly yelled out to me, "Get your flashlight!"

I pulled the LED penlight out and turned it on, which only made matters worse momentarily while it reflected off the inside surface of the cart onto the Lexan windshield!

I leaned out of the cart and scanned the grassy meadow for my site. Sure enough, the reflectors on my Electra Glide were a telltale sign of where Curly needed to steer the cart. His RV was well-lit, so after dropping me off, he had a clear shot to his front door.

There had been nearly a full moon earlier in the evening, but it was then pitch-black in camp. Curly shouldn't have needed any light at all were it not for the cloud cover that had rolled in.

I nearly sweat to death in the ninety-something heat and prairie humidity when I had pitched camp and dreaded the thought of lying awake in a hot nylon cocoon while trying to sleep.

However, the cause for the ink-black night was also responsible for a comfortable night's sleep. While the clouds from the front that rolled in obscured the moon completely, the front also brought extremely high winds, which blew across the open vents beneath the tent fly, making it quite cool. In fact, I ended up crawling in my sleeping bag around 3:00 a.m. to escape the then fifty-something prairie wind.

I was awoken before light by a jingling sound of some sort just outside my tent—somebody's dog was loose. After the fourth time it drove its nose into the sheer nylon wall of my new tent, I whacked it on the snout and yelled loudly. I heard the jingling from the dog tags fade in the distance as it ran off. I hated scaring the poor thing, but I didn't want a hole through my tent wall either.

I awoke around sunup and crawled out about 5:45 a.m. Although my bad leg from last September's crash was very stiff and uncooperative first thing in the morning, I decided to walk up the hill to the Last Chance gas stop / C-store for breakfast.

They had prewrapped breakfast sandwiches, which couldn't have been more than three years old! I grabbed a ham-egg-and-cheese specimen and ate in the little grove of picnic benches across from the store, overlooking I-90, which is deserted at that hour of the day.

After choking down that nasty sandwich, I walked back down the hill to break camp. No one else in camp was awake yet as I restuffed my sleeping bag, sheet, and mini-My Pillow into their stuff sacks.

As I was ready to break down the tent, I had a visitor. The dog that woke me earlier had returned. It was a Rottweiler puppy, apparently starved for affection. It kept standing on my feet or leaning on my legs, looking up at me, expecting me to pet it or something!

I worked around that stagnant lump of dog flesh until it almost caused me to trip. Despite yelling loudly at him to go, he just kept wagging his tail in my way, no matter on which side of the tent I was pulling stakes or guy lines. I finally got the tent into its bag, despite my "supervisor," but when I attempted to turn over the ground sheet onto which the tent was placed, the damn puppy marched right into the middle of it and plopped down! What the hell!

I took hold of two corners of the plastic sheet and yanked it as hard as I could. Sure enough, I succeeded in stripping the sheet from under the dog, kind of like where somebody tries to yank a table cloth, leaving all the place settings intact. Only it didn't work out so well for puppy.

Apparently there was enough friction between his underbelly and the ground cloth that when I pulled it out from under him, he didn't slide like I had hoped. Instead, he rolled repeatedly. He must have instinctively put his legs out while rolling because when the cloth finally cleared him, he was standing upright!

I roared laughing. The dog was perplexed apparently. He looked at the ground, then cocked his head and looked at me. He did that four times before letting out a sigh before settling back on his stomach again. Talk about priceless dog expressions. Man, that was funny!

After I had packed all the gear into the bike, I grabbed my shaving kit and headed off to the showers with puppy on my heels. *Hmm…perhaps I could lock him in and leave him behind?* I wondered. I didn't need a dog jumping in front of the bike when I rolled out.

Against my better judgment, I didn't imprison puppy, who followed me back to my bike, almost tripping me a second time.

Because the last things I had to secure on the bike went into the Tour Pak (rear of the bike), puppy decided to settle down in the grass behind the rear wheel. I was getting really annoyed. I couldn't safely navigate across the loose gravel, then muddy lane, if puppy decided to pace the bike. That makes for a high probability for dumping a nine hundred-plus-pound bike and its forty-five- to fifty-pound contents by a guy with a bad left leg.

Well, as fate would have it, on starting the big V-twin, puppy was blasted from behind the bike by the dual exhaust thrust. He tore ass across the campground and dove into some bushes, far from me and the bike! Heh heh heh, skeered the little fella.

By then, it was almost eight o'clock as I rolled into the brisk prairie air. It was cool enough for my leathers, but I knew from many years' experience that it would warm up before too long. So I did without.

Unlike the day before of Super Slab riding to Gillette, I put on a helmet. Riding the shoulder-less two-lanes through deer- and antelope-infested prairie has the potential for the *need for* a helmet—enough said.

I hate riding the Super Slab where there's any alternative two-lane road, but in that stretch of eastern Wyoming and western South Dakota, there isn't—at least not in the direction I was headed. But at that hour, there was almost no one else on I-90. I made it to the Spearfish-Belle Fourche exit in no time and headed north on US 85—the Can Am Highway. Before long, the all-knowing GPS diverted me onto SD 79. Up in that stretch of America, there isn't much to encounter—just miles and miles of grassland prairie as far as one can see. The landscape there is broken up occasionally by one-room gothic wooden churches, abandoned frame houses, and giant rolls of hay. Once in a great while, I would spot a tractor off in the distance cutting hay or herds of Herefords but little else. It's more remote up there than much of Wyoming.

Surprisingly, the temperature up there never broke eighty, in contrast to the upper nineties along the Wyoming high plains the day before. It was pleasant riding without seeing other vehicles for ten to twenty miles at a stretch.

Never listen to your GPS alone. Always listen to your gut instinct and memory. I failed to heed that advice, and it cost me. I dropped the new bike!

And that is when I learned Paul just might be right about buying a lighter Harley.

I was rolling along at sixty-five miles an hour approaching yet another of the many dog-leg turnoffs on the road up in North Dakota within about thirty miles of Golden Valley, my destination. I knew where I had to make my turn, but with my brain on autopilot, I listened to the GPS when that sexy bitch told me, "Turn right, *now.*"

I crushed the brakes, bleeding off speed from sixty-five to barely a crawl. However, I didn't slow in time enough to turn into the right side of the lane leading into the small town where I had hoped to find gas. Instead, I attempted a tight "police U-turn," which I've done successfully hundreds of times. When maneuvering at such low speed, you never look down. (If you look down, you go down.) Instead, you keep your head up, looking over your shoulder where you want the bike to go. You slip the clutch until you straighten out when it's safe to pick up speed. The only problem was, the left side of the lane was covered in tiny gravel, too small and too much like the road to see even if I had looked down. At the extreme lean angle required to execute the police U-turn, that gravel was like ball bearings. The bike went out from under me before I could even get my foot off the running board. My ankle was clamped momentarily between the folded-up running board and the bike, which caused me to auger my right knee into the asphalt. Screw me!

I was thrust clear of the bike and braced my fall instinctively with my right hand, but it suffered no trauma because I wear leather gloves while riding. But man, my skin was sheared from my knee even though my jeans never tore. The worst part was, I was pretty sure I had just fractured my ankle!

My brain was screaming at me, "Shake it off, right the bike, and press on!" That is exactly what I attempted to do, but results weren't forthcoming.

I haven't had to pick up an Electra Glide since 2005. I was straddling that bike, reaching around the fairing to adjust the spot lamps on the then-brand-new '05. My leg must have pushed the kickstand back enough to miss the lock notch. The bike started to lean to the left, so I put my hands on the grips to ease it onto the kickstand. But it folded up, and the bike went down. I had the Tour Pak open because I was using the factory-supplied tool kit to adjust the spots. Well, when it went over, the Tour Pak cracked. That was a five-hundred-dollar mistake! I hadn't dropped another bike since until moments earlier, despite coming close on muddy roads a few times.

Electra Glides cannot fall all the way over onto their side. Instead, they rest on the engine guard bar up front and the saddlebag guard bar in the rear. But even at that angle, you cannot actually "pick it up." Instead, for a right-side drop, you put your left hand on the right grip and your other hand on the passenger grab rail, and then you squat down low and walk backward. In other words, you lift the bike with your legs. That's a tall order for a seven hundred-plus-pound '05 Electra Glide, but after a couple of attempts, I righted that bike easily.

Unfortunately, the new 2019 weighs over nine hundred pounds. Furthermore, it was loaded with tools, clothes, and camping gear, with a good bit strapped high up on the Tour Pak rack. Lifting this bike would be a challenge.

It's always better when a bike falls to the right side so you can put the kickstand down on the left to prevent it from falling back over if you cannot control the right-side lift. I went down on the right, so that was in my favor, at least.

I set the kickstand, verified the transmission was in gear, and then walked around to the right side, ready to right the bike.

However, Harley no longer puts passenger grab rails on the latest Electra Glides. I tried to leverage the much lower top of the saddle-bag guard rail but couldn't get a good grip. Still, I grabbed what I could and started to walk back, but I wasn't going anywhere.

My left leg is still recovering, and I had just crushed my right ankle when the bike went down. I simply couldn't get a good purchase to walk the bike upright, despite trying for nearly twenty minutes. What else was I going to do in the treeless, shadeless prairie with no one else in sight?

I decided to unload the bike and sweep as much fine gravel and sand away from where my feet had to go when I heard a vehicle approaching, although I couldn't see it yet over the rolling terrain. Once I saw the pickup, I waved down the driver, hoping he would stop. Luckily, he did.

I asked him to help me right the bike, and he agreed. Once I explained to him what not to grab onto, we got her up easily. Man, I was grateful and told him so repeatedly.

When the man saw me limping, he asked whether I needed medical help. I explained to him my limp is from the crash I had in September, which was mostly true. My right ankle, however, was screaming at me from this minor spill.

I also asked the man where I could get gas. Despite getting 52.1 miles per gallon at sixty-five miles an hour, I was near empty—I should have topped off in Beulah! I hadn't seen a gas station since Belle Fourche. (I later discovered that it's 104 miles between gas stations along my chosen route.) The man directed me to a small town eighteen miles out of my way. I thanked him again and waved as he rode off.

Before I could get back under way, I had to move the highway peg bracket that had folded up under the rear brake pedal. I did that easily with the tools I always have with me on the bike. The bracket suffered some scratches and probably protected the bike from further damage. Only the undersides of the guard bars showed evidence of the drop, and most of that wiped off because the bike slid only on the gravel and fine sandy soil beneath it.

The worst damage suffered was not to the bike or even my ankle. My pride was in critical condition after making that rookie mistake!

I could blame the GPS or any number of other factors, but the fact remains: I screwed up. I should have looked down to scan the road surface *before* attempting the tight, steep-angle turn, *or* I should have come to a complete stop before making a normal take-off-from-stop. But I hadn't—and I paid for it!

Anyway, the bike was fine, and I would heal once more. But I became really concerned whether I could pick that bike up by myself after *all* my injuries were healed—else it might be time for a Tri-Glide trike! *Damn it, Paul, you might be right!* I thought.

I followed the man's directions to the dead end from where I had to make a left into Stanton, North Dakota, for gas. When I applied the brakes at the junction, my right ankle pain was significant. When I put my feet down at the stop, however, the pressure on my ankle was unbearable. It might not have been broken fully, but it was a sure thing it was fractured!

I rolled on into Stanton from US 12 and found the Cenex fuel depot, which served mainly diesel for all the farm equipment staged at the pumps. Once I was able to get up to the pumps, all I saw was eighty-seven octane. The fuel-injected Harley requires ninety-one minimum, else risk engine-destroying pre-detonation.

I pulled away from the pumps and rode around town, looking for another station. But after about six blocks later—the whole of Stanton—I wound up back at the Cenex. Luckily, I came into the opposite side of the island from my first pass, on which there was a single ninety-one octane pump. I squeezed every drop I could get into that six-gallon tank.

I then had to make a decision: press on or head back to Cody, 525 miles away. Because my ankle hurt so badly while standing at the pump and because I saw *nowhere* to camp or to get a room for the night north of Belle Fourche, I decided to ride straight back to Cody. And even if I camped somewhere closer to I-90, I was concerned whether I would be able get my right boot back on in the morning if my ankle swelled overnight. The die had been cast on dropping the bike—I would have to run tankful to tankful straight home. And that's just what I did.

I hit the road a little before 8:00 a.m. the preceding day and parked in the garage just before 8:00 p.m. the next night with 1,100 miles under my belt. All that riding in those two days was for nothing. I was within 30 to 40 miles of my intended destination when I aborted my trip. That just pissed me off! But I only had myself to blame.

It's always good to get home to Stacey, so my aborted trip wasn't a total loss. And besides, she helped me ice down my ankle.

So was that turn of events karma for not petting that love-starved Rottweiler? I have no idea. Nevertheless, I can tell you this: if any other wayward pooch nuzzles me for some affection while I'm on another road trip, I'll be sure to pet him…just in case!

AFTERMATH

It was gratifying to learn that the preceding collection of on-the-road tales was accepted for publication. While this is not the first time I have been published, it's the first time I've drawn solely on first-hand real-life experiences. This is a milestone of sorts for me because it provides closure to something that happened when I was in tenth grade—I had gotten an F in English, which was totally undeserved. So how did I go from that failure to being published?

Let me explain.

The first day of English class in tenth grade with *that bitch* Mrs. Lonia was very telling. She stood in front of the class and stated, "All my girls always do well. You boys just don't seem to get it." I didn't think much of that comment at the time, but little did I know that I and other guys in that class were going to be blatantly discriminated against by that sexist douchebag!

Most of tenth grade English focused on composition. I never achieved a grade better than a D+ on any paper that I turned in that year. I was frustrated and completely ashamed. Even the term paper that I had worked so hard on—after doing hours of library research, recording facts supported with references, drawing logical conclusions, and presenting it precisely and concisely—"earned" me an F! I was devastated.

If all of that weren't bad enough, I got an F for English for my final grade, and I was then destined for summer school! My parents were pissed off—not only over the failing grade but over the logistics of getting me to school for class. There was no bus transportation for summer school, and Dad drove to work every day with the only car we had because Mom didn't drive.

So I ended up walking the four-and-a-half miles every day. After all, I had failed, right? Shouldn't I have to pay a price? At least that was my mindset on accepting the realization that—apparently—I couldn't write worth shit!

I'll never forget what my summer school teacher, Mr. McCann, said to me on handing back our papers after our first take-home writing assignment. Mine had no grade written on it, unlike all the others that he returned.

He pulled me aside and said quietly, "You didn't write this, did you?"

I was in shock. Before I could collect my thoughts and answer him, he went on.

"Who wrote this for you? There are phrases, expressions, and construct in here that are too mature to have come from you."

"I swear, Mr. McCann, I wrote it. Nobody helped me. I don't know how I can prove it to you, but—"

He interrupted, "Well, I'm not giving you a grade for this now. We'll just have to see how you do on the next few assignments."

My heart was racing. I'd just been accused of a "crime" I didn't commit and with no way to prove it. I suddenly became fearful I might get held back and have to repeat tenth grade. Screw me!

For whatever reason, Mr. McCann believed I had plagiarized my paper. I had to prove to him somehow that I had completed that writing assignment without any help. But at least he hadn't *concluded* that I submitted someone else's work as my own; he left the door open for the possibility that I was actually the author on telling me that he wouldn't grade my paper "now."

For my second take-home assignment, the outcome was nearly the same—he pulled me aside and told me didn't believe I had crafted my paper, although that time he expressed doubts. However, his doubts were based only on the fact that I had failed English composition and shouldn't be in his class if I truly could turn in work that, to him, was acceptable—albeit suspect.

My face must have lit up on learning our next assignment was to be written in class. I could vindicate myself by turning in an assignment, crafted under McCann's nose, where I couldn't possibly have someone else do it for me or contribute.

So the day of the assignment, I was prepared. I had picked a Mark Twain book (my favorite author) to be the subject of my report. The allotted three and a half hours was just enough to finish editing and polishing my paper before submitting to Mr. McCann. Well, whether good or bad, that time at least, he would know that what I had turned in was mine.

Shit! Are you kidding me? I thought as Mr. McCann once again called me aside at the start of the next class. But that time, I would relish what he had to say.

"There's no way you should have failed English! I don't understand why you're in my class. Anyway, I've now graded your first three assignments."

He handed me my papers. At the top of each one, written in red ink, was a large A+.

I knew it! I knew that bitch Lonia screwed me, I thought. I had never struggled to write ever since I started journaling in grade school. I didn't always earn an A+—there were a few Bs from time to time—but I damn sure wasn't an F-student!

I've also never forgotten what Mr. McCann told me that day after our third assignment or how he did right by me: he waited for objective proof rather than simply conclude that I hadn't been turning in my own work. After completing that third assignment, under his watchful eye, that removed all doubt, and then he gave me the grades that he felt I had earned.

I aced every other writing project that Mr. McCann assigned that summer. As fate would have it, he was also my eleventh grade English teacher on recommencing classes that September. Throughout eleventh grade, every writing assignment I turned in to Mr. McCann was returned with no less than an A-.

In senior year, I elected to take Advanced Placement English, but only because by doing that, I wasn't required to turn in a lengthy term paper. Our family didn't have a set of encyclopedias, and so doing a paper on a topic that I couldn't research easily would have been disastrous. However, AP English required that I read a different book *each week* and turn in a book report.

We had a real suck-tail brown-noser in my AP class named Sandy. She was definitely a smart Honor Society student, yet despite that, she would stroke our teachers' egos to earn brownie points anyway she could and in the most blatant, transparent ways imaginable. For example, she asked our teacher Mr. Latshaw whether he preferred single or double spaces for her typed book reports (which her secretary mom cranked out for her). The rest of us turned in hand-written reports. Mine were probably the worst for readability.

In tenth grade, Sandy had also been one of Mrs. Lonia's girls-on-a-pedestal, who could do no wrong. I hated her!

In high school, I procrastinated terribly, which, I believed back then, made me a better writer because unless I had deadline pressure, the words just wouldn't flow. So I never started any of my reports before midnight of the day they were due, often finishing after 4:00 a.m. They looked awful, completed with all of the scribbled-out edits. I had no time to rewrite from scratch after editing if I were to make the school bus on time. I only got away with that because Mr. Latshaw was a very cool teacher.

In spring of senior year, I took my AP exams and tested out of the six required college English writing credits. But the best part was throughout the year, I scored higher grades on every assignment than those that Sandy earned with her double-spaced, type-written, folder-bound essays against my hand-written, scribbled messes. I got straight As; Sandy didn't!

So it would seem that Mrs. Lonia really did have a hard-on against guys, but there was no real proof. One could argue that I simply had had an off year, despite my demonstrated writing facility before and after tenth grade.

When I was twenty-two, I worked with a guy, Mark, who had also attended my high school but graduated several years before me. One day we were chatting about stuff from our school days and some of the teachers we had. Man, you'd a thought I booted him in the ass when I mentioned Mrs. Lonia!

Very nearly the same thing that had happened to me had happened to him, only Mark's parents challenged Lonia's assessment of his first writing assignment, which earned him a D-. They demanded—and got—a meeting with Principal Turner, who had once been an English teacher himself. Mr. Turner told Mark and his parents that he wouldn't have graded his paper any less than a B+ and seemed quite perturbed at Lonia. Turner had Mark assigned to another English class, where he excelled for the rest of the year.

I then wondered how many other students of that hateful bitch had their grade averages pulled down because of her. No one will ever know.

What I do know is that I rebounded from that horrible teacher and have the writing credit to prove it.

So screw you, Mrs. Lonia!

And now you know the rest of the story.

ABOUT THE AUTHOR

 Jay Barratt has been recording his true-life experiences among his many interests—bicycling, camping, rock hounding, hiking, fishing, and, especially, motorcycling—since he began journaling in grade school. He has traveled cross-country repeatedly—in the saddle of his Harley-Davidson motorcycles—meeting many memorable characters along the way, and he has survived many amusing and sometimes harrowing experiences too.

During his professional career, Jay authored numerous technical articles and procedures. Now in retirement, Jay has the time to write about things that interest him—mostly his motorcycling adventures of the past forty-plus years. Jay has been riding Harleys since 1978 and has over 630,000 motorcycle miles under his belt, which has resulted in countless journal pages covering a lifetime of over-the-road adventures.

There's Always More Fun to Be Had! provides the reader a glimpse of some of the "big fun" that can only be had from the saddle of a Harley—although you don't need to be a biker to share in the fun!

Jay lives in Park County, Wyoming, with his wife, Stacey, who has supported—and participated in—his biker lifestyle for the past thirty years. If there is anything Jay and Stacey have learned together, it's that…there is always more fun to be had!

You can contact Jay at jay.barratt.wy@gmail.com.

CPSIA information can be obtained
at www.ICGtesting.com
Printed in the USA
BVHW090607161121
621700BV00016B/541

9 781662 446726